STECK-VAUGHN

BOOK 2

Entry to English Literacy

A Real-Life Approach

Teacher's Edition

C0-CZR-557

Author

Kathleen Kelley Beal

Reviewers

Beth Powell
Literacy Specialist
Houston Community College

Kathleen Santopietro
Consultant, Adult Basic Education
Colorado Department of Education

STECK-VAUGHN
COMPANY
A Subsidiary of National Education Corporation

Acknowledgments

About the Author

Kathleen Kelley Beal is an experienced educator in the field of English as a Second Language. She has taught ESL at the University of Colorado in Boulder, Colorado; at Fort Steilacoom Community College in Tacoma, Washington; and at Mott Community College in Flint, Michigan. She has served as consultant and presenter at many ESL workshops and conferences and is the author of *Speaking of Pictures*, a conversation-oriented program for adult ESL students.

Photography

Cover: © Richard Laird / FPG

Illustration

Linda Butler

Staff Credits

Supervising Editor: Carolyn M. Hall
Senior Editor: Beverly A. Grossman
Design: Scott Huber
Cover Design: Joyce Spicer, Assistant Art Director

ISBN 0-8114-4636-0

Copyright © 1991 Steck-Vaughn Company
All rights reserved. No part of the material protected by this copyright may be reproduced or utilized in any form or by any means, electronic or mechanical, including photocopying, recording, or by any information storage and retrieval system, without permission in writing from the copyright owner. Requests for permission to make copies of any part of the work should be mailed to: Copyright Permissions, Steck-Vaughn Company, P.O. Box 26015, Austin, TX 78755. Printed in the United States of America.

1 2 3 4 5 6 7 8 9 0   HG   96 95 94 93 92 91

Contents

Overview

Entry to English Literacy is a preliteracy stepping-stone to the *Real-Life English* program. It is designed to be used with the ever-increasing number of adult students who enter English as a Second Language programs with little or no literacy training in their first language.

Entry to English Literacy starts at the zero level to form a bridge for students between preliteracy and functional English. The emphasis in this series is on reading and writing rather than conversation, although oral/aural skills naturally become part of any ESL program.

All vocabulary within the activities is adult-appropriate. In general, the activities are meaningful to adults and relate to their real world. Students are actively involved in constructing their own knowledge. In *Book 2*, student-produced language is used to practice sight words and phonics.

Adults learn best by association and doing. Teacher-directed learning is often less effective than actively involving the students in their own learning process. Personalizing the material as much as possible will help these students connect what they are learning to what they face everyday.

This sense of connection is accomplished through activities that draw upon students' experiences. Frequently students are asked to tell their experiences as they relate to the skill being learned, with whatever language capacity they possess. These experiences are written in the form of their Language Experience Story (LES). Accept the LES story exactly the way the student tells it to you. If the teacher tries to "improve" on the wording, it may not be what the students really want to say and they may not relate to it. Students will more likely be able to read their own wording and, in turn, will be able to write their story. At first students may express only two or three words. As their vocabulary and sentence structure skills gradually improve, however, students will recognize that reading and writing has personal meaning and value for them.

Using the Books

Suggestions for using *Entry to English* are printed in the *Teacher's Edition*. Only printed matter to which students have been introduced is included in the pupil's edition.

A variety and combination of teaching techniques are suggested. Variety is the key rather than specific technique. The most important point is that the teacher feels comfortable with his or her approach and involves the students personally. *How* teaching methods are used is more important than *what* method is used. Different circumstances demand different approaches. Emergency words, signs and symbols, and personal data are taught best as sight words/whole words and in the context of an actual situation. Later, students will benefit from exposure to phonic skills.

Concepts are presented logically, one skill building on another, and reinforced through exercises, games, activities, and by writing the Language Experience Story. The exercises may be repeated as many times as the teacher considers desirable. Skills should be adequately reinforced before students can internalize them. Review exercises are frequently included to achieve this goal.

Each page of teacher notes includes a statement of **Objective**, the requisite **Preparation** needed for the lesson being addressed, and the **Presentation**. The **Presentation** section may include demonstration strategies, comprehension checks, practice, and assessment of the skill.

Suggestions are provided for pre-teaching new vocabulary so that a lesson will not be interrupted with unfamiliar words. Avoid presenting words in isolation. Suggestions are also given for students to keep a notebook along with the pupil text. Activities for each notebook page correspond with the appropriate pupil page.

The use of an overhead projector can be helpful to introduce each lesson and for students to use as a model while they complete a lesson. The overhead projector is suggested as an option. You may find use of a chalkboard to be equally effective.

About the Preliterate Student

Many adult learners are highly motivated; some of these learners, however, may need special attention before learning can take place. Some students have never held a pencil or used a book. By not assuming that the student has any basic skills, the teacher can avoid student embarrassment and anxiety. The student will be more comfortable if instruction starts at the absolute beginning level: how to hold a pencil and how to position the paper/book. Students who have already mastered these basic skills will benefit from review.

Peer assistance is encouraged at all times. Students will feel more comfortable if they are not asked to perform alone. Suggestions are frequently made to have students work in small groups. This kind of activity allows them to feel more confident and relaxed. Each small group may have a group leader/facilitator who is capable of leading group exercises. This leader could be a more advanced student who would benefit by serving in a leadership capacity. Other group members will be encouraged by this procedure as well.

Teachers can contribute greatly to building a student's self-concept by calling students by their names, exercising patience, showing respect, repeating directions, etc. The classroom's physical atmosphere is important, too. Displaying the students' work makes students feel that their efforts are important and worthwhile.

Self-esteem and confidence are necessary to students' growth and progress at any level, but these qualities are especially essential at the zero level of performance.

Aa	Argentina	any	Africa
	America	are	make
	Alaska	Saudi Arabia	army
Bb	Brazil	big	back
	able	Baltimore	Burma
	about	Boston	cable
Cc	can	China	Cuba
	Costa Rica	Canada	Cambodia
	car	California	march
Dd	Dayna	Detroit	good
	do	did	Dallas
	December	Dwight	done
Ee	Ethiopia	end	Easter
	made	England	even
	Egypt	each	eager
Ff	far	France	Florida
	life	first	for
	San Francisco	Friday	leaf
Gg	Greece	again	group
	going	Georgia	Germany
	get	Gary	began

OBJECTIVES

Students will identify the uppercase and lowercase letters *A-G* in written words. Students will review page numbers 1-100.

PREPARATION

Create a set of uppercase and lowercase alphabet flash cards for each group of four students. Provide, or have each student bring, a spiral notebook with at least 100 pages.

PRESENTATION

1. Use the uppercase and lowercase *A-G* flash cards to play Concentration. Place the cards face down on a table for each small group. Ask individuals from each group, one at a time, to turn over two cards. When they turn over two cards that match, such as uppercase *A* and lowercase *a,* they keep the cards. If the cards don't match, they return them to the table face down in the same position in which they were found. Members of each group work together. Keep playing until all cards are matched. The group that matches all the letters first wins the game.

2. On pupil page 1, model circling the uppercase and lowercase letters in each row that match the letters on the left. Ask the students to do the same in their texts.

3. Ask students to write their names, addresses, and phone numbers on the front of their notebooks. Ask them to number the notebook pages at the bottom from 1-100. Circulate to check for comprehension. When all students have completed the numbering, have the class count the pages in unison.

4. Write words on the chalkboard that students learned in Book 1, such as *name, quarter, penny,* or *address.* Have the students copy the words in their spiral notebooks on page 1. Ask them to do the same with random words from pupil page 1. This exercise is for letter recognition only, but positive comments should be given to students who recognize words.

OBJECTIVES

Students will identify the uppercase and lowercase letters *H-N* in written words.

PREPARATION

Bring the alphabet flash cards.

PRESENTATION

1. Use the uppercase and lowercase *H-N* flash cards to play Concentration. Place the cards face down on a table for each small group. Ask individuals from each group, one at a time, to turn over two cards. When they turn over two cards that match, such as uppercase *H* and lowercase *h*, they keep the cards. If the cards don't match, they return them to the table face down in the same position in which they were found. Members of each group work together. Keep playing until all cards are matched. The group that matches all the letters first wins the game.

2. On pupil page 2, model circling the uppercase and lowercase letters in each row that match the letters on the left. Ask the students to do the same in their texts. Since the first four pages of *Entry to English Literacy Book 2* follow the same pattern, the students should quickly realize that they can complete pages 2 through 4 just as they completed page 1. Prediction plays a major role in becoming a reader. When material is familiar, there is far less risk that students will make mistakes. Students, therefore, move ahead more rapidly. Several sections of *Entry to English Literacy Book 2* will include material that is predictable due to repetition.

3. Write words on the chalkboard that students learned in Book 1, such as *name, quarter, penny,* or *address*. Have the students copy the words in their spiral notebooks on page 2. Ask them to do the same with random words from pupil page 2. This exercise is for letter recognition only, but positive comments should be given to students who recognize words.

Hh	Haiti	she	hand
	Hawaii	holiday	Hong Kong
	such	had	hollow
Ii	in	like	Indonesia
	Indian	i	Illinois
	Iran	find	insect
Jj	judge	join	June
	Judy	Japan	job
	just	Juan	jury
Kk	Kelley	make	Kuwait
	Kenya	know	take
	Korea	kind	blink
Ll	Libya	Louisiana	Los Angeles
	all	look	let
	last	Laos	tile
Mm	Monday	Mexico	name
	number	Minneapolis	mom
	Meng	moon	money
Nn	November	any	long
	Neng	next	never
	Nicaragua	Navajo	ant

2

Oo	Ohio	Oregon	do
	got	of	October
	Olga	on	only
Pp	Poland	help	open
	Philippines	place	put
	Pacific	Philip	popular
Qq	Quebec	Queen	Quincy
	quarter	quiet	question
	quick	Quito	quill
Rr	right	room	your
	Russia	Ricardo	work
	river	Rhodesia	silver
Ss	Sweden	must	Spanish
	Siang	South America	saw
	so	's	sing
Tt	Taiwan	Tennessee	the
	into	Thailand	Tien
	take	out	total
Uu	Utah	put	you
	use	United States	rural
	Uruguay	nut	Europe

OBJECTIVES

Students will identify the uppercase and lowercase letters *O-U* in written words.

PREPARATION

Bring the alphabet flash cards. Make several photocopies of a page from a book with large print.

PRESENTATION

1. Use the uppercase and lowercase *O-U* flash cards to play Concentration. Place the cards face down on a table for each small group. Ask individuals from each group, one at a time, to turn over two cards. When they turn over two cards that match, such as uppercase *O* and lowercase *o*, they keep the cards. If the cards don't match, they return them to the table face down in the same position in which they were found. Members of each group work together. Keep playing until all cards are matched. The group that matches all the letters first wins the game.

2. On pupil page 2, model circling the uppercase and lowercase letters in each row that match the letters on the left. Ask the students to do the same in their texts.

3. Distribute the photocopied pages. Ask the students to circle any letters *O-U*. Have the students exchange pages to verify that no letters were missed.

4. Write words on the chalkboard that students learned in Book 1, such as *Date of Birth,* or *Color of Eyes.* Have the students copy the words in their spiral notebooks on page 3. Ask them to do the same with random words from pupil page 3. This exercise is for letter recognition only, but positive comments should be given to students who recognize words.

OBJECTIVES

Students will identify the uppercase and lowercase letters *V-Z* in written words.

PREPARATION

Bring the alphabet flash cards. Make several photocopies of a magazine or newspaper advertisement with large print.

PRESENTATION

1. Use the uppercase and lowercase *V-Z* flash cards to play Concentration. Place the cards face down on a table for each small group. Ask individuals from each group, one at a time, to turn over two cards. When they turn over two cards that match, such as uppercase *V* and lowercase *v*, they keep the cards. If the cards don't match, they return them to the table face down in the same position in which they were found. Members of each group work together. Keep playing until all cards are matched. The group that matches all the letters first wins the game.

2. At the top of pupil page 4, model circling the uppercase and lowercase letters in each row that match the letters on the left. Ask the students to do the same in their texts.

3. At the bottom of pupil page 4, model circling the uppercase and lowercase letters in words in the sentences that match the letters on the left. Ask the students to do the same in their texts.

4. Distribute the photocopied ads. Ask the students to circle any letters *V-Z*. Have the students exchange pages to verify that no letters were missed.

5. Write words on the chalkboard that students learned in Book 1, such as *Phone,* or *Color of Hair.* Have the students copy the words in their spiral notebooks on page 4. Ask them to do the same with random words from pupil page 4. This exercise is for letter recognition only, but positive comments should be given to students who recognize words.

Vv	Vermont	every	Vietnam
	Venezuela	vegetable	very
	even	Vang	vain
Ww	Washington	when	water
	was	Wendy	West Virginia
	what	Wednesday	windy
Xx	Xavier	box	ax
	oxen	X-ray	tax
	Xenia	Xanthus	extra
Yy	Yang	Yugoslavia	your
	Yemen	York	fly
	yet	year	toy
Zz	Zurich	zone	Zamora
	dozen	zipper	Zaire
	zero	Zambia	lazy

Dd Did Dayna and Dwight get back in October?

Ee Easter is celebrated in England and France.

Mm Next Monday Neng will get a new number.

also	h y (a) p (l) t (s) h (o)
like	a (l) z (i) u (k) (e) j m
they	(t) s (h) q (e) (y) n v d
Laos	(L) F p (a) c (o) v (s) e
very	(v) o (e) q (r) d g f (y)
with	(w) u (i) l (t) m r x (h)
FIRE	T (F) L (I) H (R) B (E) D
face	(f) l (a) r (c) a (e) h n
EXIT	(E) F S J (X) (I) L (T) D
OPEN	D (O) (P) D (E) F M (N) M
WORK	(W) V M (O) C (R) N H (K)
NAME	(N) M H (A) N (M) N F (E)

OBJECTIVE

Students will be able to identify the individual letters that make up a given word.

PREPARATION

Bring the alphabet flash cards and tape.

PRESENTATION

1. Point to the word *also* at the top of the left hand column of pupil page 5. Ask the students to name the individual letters in the word. Then demonstrate that the same letters have been circled in the row to the right. Demonstrate tracing over the four circles. Emphasize you are circling the same letters contained in the word on the left. Point to the incorrect letters one at a time and shake your head. Now point to the correct letters and nod. Ask the students to complete the remaining rows in their texts.

2. Create groups of four students. On the chalkboard, reproduce four of the rows from pupil page 5, or create new ones. Ask the members of group #1 to come to the chalkboard. Have each group member circle the letters that spell the word on the left. Ask the class to verify the group's responses. Continue with the next group and four new rows.

3. Give each group a set of flash cards. Write a random three-letter word on the chalkboard. Be sure no letters are repeated. Have each group select the cards containing the letters on the chalkboard. Then have the groups arrange the cards in correct sequence. Circulate to check for comprehension. Continue the exercise using four- and five-letter words.

4. Ask two groups to come to the chalkboard with their sets of flash cards. Give each group a roll of tape. Write a random word on the chalkboard. Have each group select the correct letters and tape them to the chalkboard. The first group to complete the word wins. Leave the words on the chalkboard and continue with two new groups. When the chalkboard is filled, ask the students to copy the words in their spiral notebooks on page 5.

OBJECTIVE

Students will be able to identify the cluster of letters that make up a given word.

PREPARATION

Bring the alphabet flash cards and tape.

PRESENTATION

1. Point to the word *also* at the top of the left hand column of pupil page 6. Ask the students to name the individual letters in the word. Then demonstrate that the same letters have been circled in the letter groups to the right. Demonstrate tracing over the circle. Emphasize you are circling the same letter order as the word on the left. Point to the incorrect letter groups one at a time and shake your head. Now point to the correct letter group and nod. Ask the students to complete the remaining columns in their texts.

2. Create groups of four students. On the chalkboard, reproduce four of the rows from pupil page 6, or create new ones. Ask the members of group #1 to come to the chalkboard. Have each group member circle the correct letter group. Ask the class to verify the group's responses. Continue with the next group and four new rows.

3. Give each group a set of flash cards. Write a random three-letter word on the chalkboard. Be sure no letters are repeated. Have each group select the cards containing the letters on the chalkboard. Then have the groups arrange the cards in correct sequence. Circulate to check for comprehension. Continue the exercise using four- and five-letter words.

4. Ask two groups to come to the chalkboard with their sets of flash cards. Give each group a roll of tape. Write a random word on the chalkboard. Have each group select the correct letters and tape them to the chalkboard. The first group to complete the word wins. Leave the words on the chalkboard and continue with two new groups. When the chalkboard is filled, ask the students to copy the words in their spiral notebooks on page 6.

also	alos	aols	(also)	aslo
like	liek	(like)	ilke	elik
they	(they)	tehy	hyte	ythe
Laos	Loas	Lsoa	(Laos)	Lsao
very	vrey	vyre	veyr	(very)
with	wthi	thiw	wiht	(with)
FIRE	ERIF	(FIRE)	FRIE	RFEI
face	(face)	fcea	feca	faec
EXIT	ETIX	XETI	(EXIT)	ITEX
OPEN	PENO	(OPEN)	OEPN	NOPE
work	wrok	wkro	(work)	rowk
name	nmae	mane	nema	(name)

Aa	L(a)oti(a)n	(a)irpl(a)ne	S(a)udi (A)r(a)bi(a)
	Sp(a)nish	c(a)ll	(A)l(a)n
Ee	Sw(e)d(e)n	P(e)rsia	t(e)ach(e)r
	j(e)t	(E)gypt	(E)nglish
Ii	(I)nd(i)an	p(i)l	Tha(i)
	wr(i)te	(I)tal(i)an	V(i)etnamese
Oo	(O)liver	(O)pen	fr(o)nt
	(O)ut	K(o)rean	Pacific (O)cean
Uu	d(u)ck	(U)ganda	(U)niversity of (U)tah
	h(u)nt	r(u)g	(U)se
Gg	Cra(g) told (G)eor(g)e to be quiet.		

1. train	h	(t)	y	(r)	l	(a)	(i)	m	(n)
2. French	E	(F)	c	(r)	(e)	b	(n)	(c)	(h)
3. BUS	D	P	(B)	R	(U)	O	Z	(S)	J

1. mail	mali	(mail)	amil	lmai
2. STOP	POST	TSOP	STPO	(STOP)
3. RIVER	RIVRE	(RIVER)	RVIER	RIVRE

OBJECTIVE
Students will review placing letters in correct sequence for word formation.

PREPARATION
On separate index cards, prepare a list of five words found around the classroom on posters, maps, ads, etc., for each group of four students. Write the words exactly the way they are found: all capitals, unique lettering, all block letters, etc.

PRESENTATION

1. Use the uppercase and lowercase *A, E, I, O, U,* and *G* flash cards to play Concentration. Place the cards face down on a table for each small group. Ask individuals from each group, one at a time, to turn over two cards. When they turn over two cards that match, such as uppercase *A* and lowercase *a,* they keep the cards. If the cards don't match, they return them to the table face down in the same position in which they were found. Members of each group work together. Keep playing until all cards are matched. The group that matches all the letters first wins the game.

2. At the top of pupil page 7, model circling the uppercase and lowercase letters in each row that match the letters on the left. Ask the students to do the same in their texts.

3. Model the second exercise on pupil page 7 by reproducing the first row on the chalkboard. Demonstrate circling the letters on the right that are contained in the word on the left. Ask the students to do the same in their texts.

4. Model the third exercise on pupil page 7 by reproducing the first row on the chalkboard. Point to the word *mail.* Ask the students to name the individual letters in the word. Then demonstrate circling the correct letter group on the right. Emphasize you are circling the same letter order as the word on the left. Point to the incorrect letter groups one at a time and shake your head. Now point to the correct letter group and nod. Ask the students to complete the remaining columns in their texts.

5. Create groups of four students. Give each group a list of five words found in the classroom. Explain that the words on the lists can be found in the classroom. Have each group check off the words as they find them. The first group to find all the words on its list wins.

OBJECTIVE

Students will associate the letter symbols *Mm* with the appropriate sound.

PREPARATION

Bring the alphabet flash cards. Prepare a set of flash cards containing the following words: *money, man, mop, map, milk, moon.* Write the letters *Aa-Zz*, each pair on a separate sheet of newsprint. Place the sheets in alphabetical order around the room.

PRESENTATION

1. Ask students to name the letter in the box at the top of pupil page 8. Have them write it several times in their spiral notebooks on page 8.

2. Hold up the *money* flash card and say *money.* Emphasize the sound of the *M.* Ask the students to repeat several times. Point from the flash card to the picture on pupil page 8 while repeating the word. Ask the students to write the word in their spiral notebooks. Repeat with the other words on the page.

3. Ask students to raise their hands if their first or last names begin with the same sound heard in the words they just learned. Write those names on the *Mm* newsprint sheet. Ask if students know any other names that begin with the *M* sound. Ask them to write those names on the chalkboard. Help them with the spelling. Underline the beginning letter. If the names don't begin with *M*, let them write the names anyway and discover that they do not begin with the correct letter. Students can erase the names that don't belong. Names that begin with *M* can be added to the newsprint. Encourage students to keep adding names or words to the newsprint wall charts where words have already been written.

4. Ask students to choose one *M* word from the chart. This word will be their key word for remembering the sound represented by *M.* Have the students write this word in their spiral notebooks on page 8. Encourage the students to illustrate the object represented by their key word.

5. Direct the students' attention to the exercise at the bottom of pupil page 8. Explain that you will dictate a list of words. If the word begins with the *M* sound, they should circle the *Mm* beside the appropriate number. If the word does *not* begin with the *M* sound, students should mark an *X* over the *Mm.* Dictate: *1. make 2. mail 3. nail 4. monkey 5. nothing 6. nose 7. most 8. mother 9. lawn.*

Aa Bb Cc Dd Ee Ff Gg Hh Ii
Jj Kk Ll [Mm] Nn Oo Pp Qq Rr
Ss Tt Uu Vv Ww Xx Yy Zz

money

man

mop

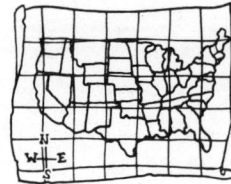
map

milk

moon

1. (Mm)   2. (Mm)   3. (X̶Mm)

4. (Mm)   5. (X̶Mm)   6. (X̶Mm)

7. (Mm)   8. (Mm)   9. (X̶Mm)

8

8

Aa Bb Cc Dd Ee Ff Gg Hh Ii
Jj Kk Ll Mm Nn Oo Pp Qq Rr
[Ss] Tt Uu Vv Ww Xx Yy Zz

sun

snow

stamp

soap

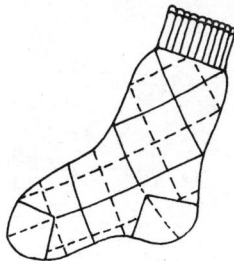

sock

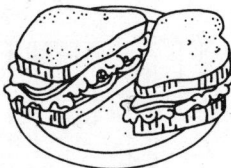

sandwich

1. (Ss)   2. ✗✗   3. (Ss)

4. (Ss)   5. ✗✗   6. (Ss)

7. ✗✗   8. (Ss)   9. ✗✗

OBJECTIVE

Students will associate the letter symbols *Ss* with the appropriate sound.

PREPARATION

Bring the alphabet flash cards. Prepare a set of flash cards containing the following words: *sun, snow, stamp, soap, sock, sandwich.*

PRESENTATION

1. Ask students to name the letter in the box at the top of pupil page 9. Have them write it several times in their spiral notebooks on page 9.

2. Hold up the *sun* flash card and say *sun.* Emphasize the sound of the S. Ask the students to repeat several times. Point from the flash card to the picture on pupil page 9 while repeating the word. Ask the students to write the word in their spiral notebooks. Repeat with the other words on the page.

3. Ask students to raise their hands if their first or last names begin with the same sound heard in the words they just learned. Write those names on the *Ss* newsprint sheet. Ask if students know any other names that begin with the *S* sound. Ask them to write those names on the chalkboard. Help them with the spelling. Underline the beginning letter. If the names don't begin with *S,* let them write the names anyway and discover that they do not begin with the correct letter. Students can erase the names that don't belong. Names that begin with *S* can be added to the newsprint. Encourage students to keep adding names or words to the newsprint wall charts where words have already been written.

4. Ask students to choose one *S* word from the chart. This word will be their key word for remembering the sound represented by *S.* Have the students write this word in their spiral notebooks on page 9. Encourage the students to illustrate the object represented by their key word.

5. Direct the students' attention to the exercise at the bottom of pupil page 9. Explain that you will dictate a list of words. If the word begins with the *S* sound, they should circle the *Ss* beside the appropriate number. If the word does *not* begin with the *S* sound, students should mark an *X* over the *Ss.* Dictate: *1. seed 2. foot 3. sit 4. sing 5. fit 6. Sue 7. zoo 8. sip 9. zip.*

OBJECTIVE

Students will associate the letter symbols *Tt* with the appropriate sound.

PREPARATION

Bring the alphabet flash cards. Prepare a set of flash cards containing the following words: *tire, toe, tape, table, taxi, teeth.*

PRESENTATION

1. Ask students to name the letter in the box at the top of pupil page 10. Have them write it several times in their spiral notebooks on page 10.

2. Hold up the *tire* flash card and say *tire.* Emphasize the sound of the *T.* Ask the students to repeat several times. Point from the flash card to the picture on pupil page 10 while repeating the word. Ask the students to write the word in their spiral notebooks. Repeat with the other words on the page.

3. Ask students to raise their hands if their first or last names begin with the same sound heard in the words they just learned. Write those names on the *Tt* newsprint sheet. Ask if students know any other names that begin with the *T* sound. Ask them to write those names on the chalkboard. Help them with the spelling. Underline the beginning letter. If the names don't begin with *T,* let them write the names anyway and discover that they do not begin with the correct letter. Students can erase the names that don't belong. Names that begin with *T* can be added to the newsprint. Encourage students to keep adding names or words to the newsprint wall charts where words have already been written.

4. Ask students to choose one *T* word from the chart. This word will be their key word for remembering the sound represented by *T.* Have the students write this word in their spiral notebooks on page 10. Encourage the students to illustrate the object represented by their key word.

5. Direct the students' attention to the exercise at the bottom of pupil page 10. Explain that you will dictate a list of words. If the word begins with the *T* sound, they should circle the *Tt* beside the appropriate number. If the word does *not* begin with the *T* sound, students should mark an *X* over the *Tt.* Dictate: *1. time 2. teacher 3. Dan 4. tongue 5. dance 6. toast 7. tan 8. boast 9. dime.*

Aa Bb Cc Dd Ee Ff Gg Hh Ii Jj Kk Ll Mm Nn Oo Pp Qq Rr Ss [Tt] Uu Vv Ww Xx Yy Zz

tire

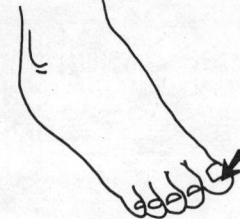
toe

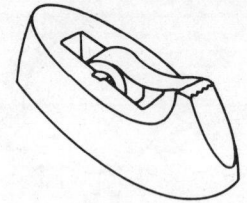
tape

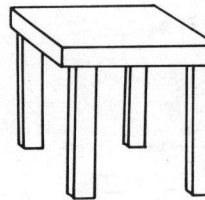
table

taxi

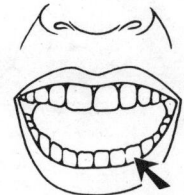
teeth

1. (Tt) 2. (Tt) 3. (X)

4. (Tt) 5. (X) 6. (Tt)

7. (Tt) 8. (X) 9. (X)

10

Aa Bb Cc Dd Ee Ff Gg Hh Ii
Jj Kk Ll Mm Nn Oo **Pp** Qq Rr
Ss Tt Uu Vv Ww Xx Yy Zz

pencil

purse

pan

piano

paddle

pot

1. (Pp)   2. (Pp)   3. X̶P̶p̶

4. (Pp)   5. (Pp)   6. X̶P̶p̶

7. X̶P̶p̶   8. (Pp)   9. X̶P̶p̶

11

OBJECTIVE

Students will associate the letter symbols *Pp* with the appropriate sound.

PREPARATION

Bring the alphabet flash cards. Prepare a set of flash cards containing the following words: *pencil, purse, pan, piano, paddle, pot.*

PRESENTATION

1. Ask students to name the letter in the box at the top of pupil page 11. Have them write it several times in their spiral notebooks on page 11.

2. Hold up the *pencil* flash card and say *pencil.* Emphasize the sound of the *P.* Ask the students to repeat several times. Point from the flash card to the picture on pupil page 11 while repeating the word. Ask the students to write the word in their spiral notebooks. Repeat with the other words on the page.

3. Ask students to raise their hands if their first or last names begin with the same sound heard in the words they just learned. Write those names on the *Pp* newsprint sheet. Ask if students know any other names that begin with the *P* sound. Ask them to write those names on the chalkboard. Help them with the spelling. Underline the beginning letter. If the names don't begin with *P,* let them write the names anyway and discover that they do not begin with the correct letter. Students can erase the names that don't belong. Names that begin with *P* can be added to the newsprint. Encourage students to keep adding names or words to the newsprint wall charts where words have already been written.

4. Ask students to choose one *P* word from the chart. This word will be their key word for remembering the sound represented by *P.* Have the students write this word in their spiral notebooks on page 11. Encourage the students to illustrate the object represented by their key word.

5. Direct the students' attention to the exercise at the bottom of pupil page 11. Explain that you will dictate a list of words. If the word begins with the *P* sound, they should circle the *Pp* beside the appropriate number. If the word does *not* begin with the *P* sound, students should mark an *X* over the *Pp.* Dictate: *1. pepper 2. pear 3. bear 4. pine 5. pig 6. fine 7. big 8. pill 9. fill.*

OBJECTIVE

Students will associate the letter symbols *Ll* with the appropriate sound.

PREPARATION

Bring the alphabet flash cards. Prepare a set of flash cards containing the following words: *lamp, ladder, lock, lemon, leaf, lizard.*

PRESENTATION

1. Ask students to name the letter in the box at the top of pupil page 12. Have them write it several times in their spiral notebooks on page 12.

2. Hold up the *lamp* flash card and say *lamp.* Emphasize the sound of the *L.* Ask the students to repeat several times. Point from the flash card to the picture on pupil page 12 while repeating the word. Ask the students to write the word in their spiral notebooks. Repeat with the other words on the page.

3. Ask students to raise their hands if their first or last names begin with the same sound heard in the words they just learned. Write those names on the bottom half of the *Ll* newsprint sheet. Ask if students know any other names that begin with the *L* sound. Ask them to write those names on the chalkboard. Help them with the spelling. Underline the beginning letter. If the names don't begin with *L,* let them write the names anyway and discover that they do not begin with the correct letter. Students can erase the names that don't belong. Names that begin with *L* can be added to the newsprint. Encourage students to keep adding names or words to the newsprint wall charts where words have already been written.

4. Ask students to choose one *L* word from the chart. This word will be their key word for remembering the sound represented by *L.* Have the students write this word in their spiral notebooks on page 12. Encourage the students to illustrate the object represented by their key word.

5. Direct the students' attention to the exercise at the bottom of pupil page 12. Explain that you will dictate a list of words. If the word begins with the *L* sound, they should circle the *Ll* beside the appropriate number. If the word does *not* begin with the *L* sound, students should mark an *X* over the *Ll.* Dictate: *1. lip 2. lake 3. rock 4. rip 5. rake 6. load 7. rail 8. road 9. woke.*

A a B b C c D d E e F f G g H h I i
J j K k ⬚Ll⬚ M m N n O o P p Q q R r
S s T t U u V v W w X x Y y Z z

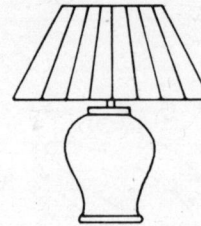

lamp

ladder

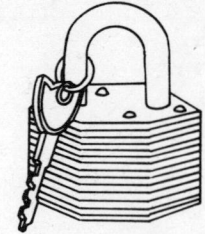

lock

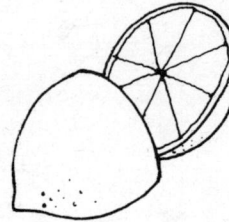

lemon

leaf

lizard

1. (Ll)   2. (Ll)   3. ⊠
4. ⊠   5. ⊠   6. (Ll)
7. ⊠   8. ⊠   9. ⊠

Aa Bb Cc Dd Ee [Ff] Gg Hh Ii
Jj Kk Ll Mm Nn Oo Pp Qq Rr
Ss Tt Uu Vv Ww Xx Yy Zz

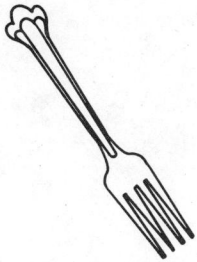

fork

fire

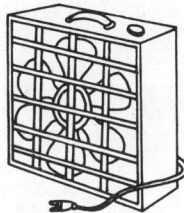

fan

finger

fish

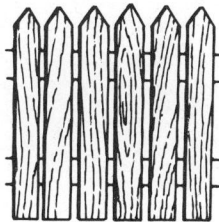

fence

1. (Ff) 2. (Ff) 3. ✗
4. ✗ 5. ✗ 6. ✗
7. (Ff) 8. (Ff) 9. (Ff)

OBJECTIVE

Students will associate the letter symbols *Ff* with the appropriate sound.

PREPARATION

Bring the alphabet flash cards. Prepare a set of flash cards containing the following words: *fork, fire, fan, finger, fish, fence.*

PRESENTATION

1. Ask students to name the letter in the box at the top of pupil page 13. Have them write it several times in their spiral notebooks on page 13.

2. Hold up the *fork* flash card and say *fork.* Emphasize the sound of the *F.* Ask the students to repeat several times. Point from the flash card to the picture on pupil page 13 while repeating the word. Ask the students to write the word in their spiral notebooks. Repeat with the other words on the page.

3. Ask students to raise their hands if their first or last names begin with the same sound heard in the words they just learned. Write those names on the bottom half of the *Ff* newsprint sheet. Ask if students know any other names that begin with the *F* sound. Ask them to write those names on the chalkboard. Help them with the spelling. Underline the beginning letter. If the names don't begin with *F,* let them write the names anyway and discover that they do not begin with the correct letter. Students can erase the names that don't belong. Names that begin with *F* can be added to the newsprint. Encourage students to keep adding names or words to the newsprint wall charts where words have already been written.

4. Ask students to choose one *F* word from the chart. This word will be their key word for remembering the sound represented by *F.* Have the students write this word in their spiral notebooks on page 13. Encourage the students to illustrate the object represented by their key word.

5. Direct the students' attention to the exercise at the bottom of pupil page 13. Explain that you will dictate a list of words. If the word begins with the *F* sound, they should circle the *Ff* beside the appropriate number. If the word does *not* begin with the *F* sound, students should mark an *X* over the *Ff.* Dictate: *1. family 2. feel 3. put 4. veal 5. nail 6. vail 7. foot 8. fail 9. fun.*

OBJECTIVE

Students will review the *M, S, T, P, L,* and *F* sounds.

PREPARATION

Photocopy the ID pictures of students whose names begin with *M, S, T, P, L,* or *F.*

PRESENTATION

1. Point to the illustration of the fish at the top of pupil page 14 and say *fish.* Emphasize the *F* sound. Ask students to fill in the missing letter. Continue with the remaining illustrations. Have the students verify each other's work.

2. At the bottom of pupil page 14, ask students to write in the blanks the uppercase and lowercase letter they hear at the beginning of each dictated word: *1. sign 2. from 3. time 4. pine 5. meat 6. face 7. leaf 8. monkey 9. sick.* Circulate to check for comprehension.

3. On notebook page 14, ask the students to copy the six consonants and the key words they chose on pages 8-13. Ask individuals to read the letters, one at a time, followed by each key word.

4. Create groups of four students. Give each group a set of photocopied ID pictures and a set of flash cards. Ask the groups to sort the pictures and place them under the letter with which the students' names begin. Ask them to write the names on the newsprint charts.

14

___*f*__ish

___*s*__oap

___*m*__ilk

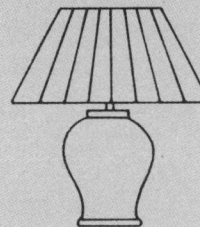
__*l*__amp

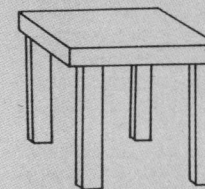
__*t*__able

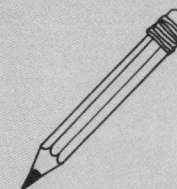
__*p*__encil

___*m*__oney

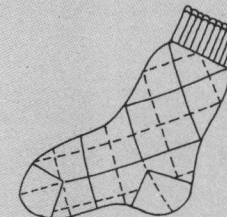
___*s*__ock

___*f*__ire

1. _____ *Ss*   2. _____ *Ff*   3. _____ *Tt*

4. _____ *Pp*   5. _____ *Mm*   6. _____ *Ff*

7. _____ *Ll*   8. _____ *Mm*   9. _____ *Ss*

14

Aa [Bb] Cc Dd Ee Ff Gg Hh Ii
Jj Kk Ll Mm Nn Oo Pp Qq Rr
Ss Tt Uu Vv Ww Xx Yy Zz

belt

bed

bench

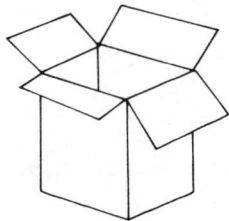

box

bus

ball

1. (Bb)   2. ⊗⊗   3. (Bb)
4. (Bb)   5. ⊗⊗   6. (Bb)
7. (Bb)   8. ⊗⊗   9. (Bb)

15

OBJECTIVE

Students will associate the letter symbols *Bb* with the appropriate sound.

PREPARATION

Bring the alphabet flash cards. Prepare a set of flash cards containing the following words: *belt, bed, bench, box, bus, ball.*

PRESENTATION

1. Ask students to name the letter in the box at the top of pupil page 15. Have them write it several times in their spiral notebooks on page 15.

2. Hold up the *belt* flash card and say *belt*. Emphasize the sound of the *B*. Ask the students to repeat several times. Point from the flash card to the picture on pupil page 15 while repeating the word. Ask the students to write the word in their spiral notebooks. Repeat with the other words on the page.

3. Ask students to raise their hands if their first or last names begin with the same sound heard in the words they just learned. Write those names on the bottom half of the *Bb* newsprint sheet. Ask if students know any other names that begin with the *B* sound. Ask them to write those names on the chalkboard. Help them with the spelling. Underline the beginning letter. If the names don't begin with *B,* let them write the names anyway and discover that they do not begin with the correct letter. Students can erase the names that don't belong. Names that begin with *B* can be added to the newsprint. Encourage students to keep adding names or words to the newsprint wall charts where words have already been written.

4. Ask students to choose one *B* word from the chart. This word will be their key word for remembering the sound represented by *B*. Have the students write this word in their spiral notebooks on page 15. Encourage the students to illustrate the object represented by their key word.

5. Direct the students' attention to the exercise at the bottom of pupil page 15. Explain that you will dictate a list of words. If the word begins with the *B* sound, they should circle the *Bb* beside the appropriate number. If the word does *not* begin with the *B* sound, students should mark an *X* over the *Bb*. Dictate: *1. baby 2. pill 3. bird 4. bill 5. push 6. ball 7. bush 8. dog 9. bus.*

OBJECTIVE

Students will associate the letter symbols *Kk* with the appropriate sound.

PREPARATION

Bring the alphabet flash cards. Prepare a set of flash cards containing the following words: *key, kitchen, kitten, kite, kettle, king.*

PRESENTATION

1. Ask students to name the letter in the box at the top of pupil page 16. Have them write it several times in their spiral notebooks on page 16.

2. Hold up the *key* flash card and say *key.* Emphasize the sound of the *K.* Ask the students to repeat several times. Point from the flash card to the picture on pupil page 16 while repeating the word. Ask the students to write the word in their spiral notebooks. Repeat with the other words on the page.

3. Ask students to raise their hands if their first or last names begin with the same sound heard in the words they just learned. Write those names on the *Kk* newsprint sheet. Ask if students know any other names that begin with the *K* sound. Ask them to write those names on the chalkboard. Help them with the spelling. Underline the beginning letter. If the names don't begin with *K,* let them write the names anyway and discover that they do not begin with the correct letter. Students can erase the names that don't belong. Names that begin with *K* can be added to the newsprint. Encourage students to keep adding names or words to the newsprint wall charts where words have already been written.

4. Ask students to choose one *K* word from the chart. This word will be their key word for remembering the sound represented by *K.* Have the students write this word in their spiral notebooks on page 16. Encourage the students to illustrate the object represented by their key word.

5. Direct the students' attention to the exercise at the bottom of pupil page 16. Explain that you will dictate a list of words. If the word begins with the *K* sound, they should circle the *Kk* beside the appropriate number. If the word does *not* begin with the *K* sound, students should mark an *X* over the *Kk.* Dictate: *1. get 2. keep 3. king 4. gill 5. go 6. kill 7. tight 8. ketchup 9. kiss.*

A a B b C c D d E e F f G g H h I i
J j [K k] L l M m N n O o P p Q q R r
S s T t U u V v W w X x Y y Z z

key

kitchen

kitten

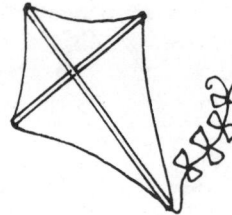

kite

kettle

king

1. ⊗̸ Kk   2. (Kk)   3. (Kk)

4. ⊗̸ Kk   5. ⊗̸ Kk   6. (Kk)

7. ⊗̸ Kk   8. (Kk)   9. (Kk)

Aa Bb Cc Dd Ee Ff Gg Hh Ii
Jj Kk Ll Mm Nn Oo Pp Qq Rr
Ss Tt Uu Vv Ww Xx Yy Zz

net

newspaper

nickel

nest

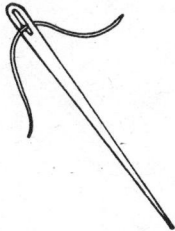

needle

nose

1. (Nn) 2. (Nn) 3. X̶N̶n̶

4. (Nn) 5. (Nn) 6. X̶N̶n̶

7. (Nn) 8. (Nn) 9. X̶N̶n̶

17

OBJECTIVE

Students will associate the letter symbols *Nn* with the appropriate sound.

PREPARATION

Bring the alphabet flash cards. Prepare a set of flash cards containing the following words: *net, newspaper, nickel, nest, needle, nose.*

PRESENTATION

1. Ask students to name the letter in the box at the top of pupil page 17. Have them write it several times in their spiral notebooks on page 17.

2. Hold up the *net* flash card and say *net.* Emphasize the sound of the *N.* Ask the students to repeat several times. Point from the flash card to the picture on pupil page 17 while repeating the word. Ask the students to write the word in their spiral notebooks. Repeat with the other words on the page.

3. Ask students to raise their hands if their first or last names begin with the same sound heard in the words they just learned. Write those names on the bottom half of the *Nn* newsprint sheet. Ask if students know any other names that begin with the *N* sound. Ask them to write those names on the chalkboard. Help them with the spelling. Underline the beginning letter. If the names don't begin with *N,* let them write the names anyway and discover that they do not begin with the correct letter. Students can erase the names that don't belong. Names that begin with *N* can be added to the newsprint. Encourage students to keep adding names or words to the newsprint wall charts where words have already been written.

4. Ask students to choose one *N* word from the chart. This word will be their key word for remembering the sound represented by *N.* Have the students write this word in their spiral notebooks on page 17. Encourage the students to illustrate the object represented by their key word.

5. Direct the students' attention to the exercise at the bottom of pupil page 17. Explain that you will dictate a list of words. If the word begins with the *N* sound, they should circle the *Nn* beside the appropriate number. If the word does *not* begin with the *N* sound, students should mark an X over the *Nn.* Dictate: *1. noodle 2. November 3. mail 4. napkin 5. nail 6. mushroom 7. not 8. need 9. meal.*

OBJECTIVE

Students will associate the letter symbols *Rr* with the appropriate sound.

PREPARATION

Bring the alphabet flash cards. Prepare a set of flash cards containing the following words: *radio, rug, roof, rain, razor, record.*

PRESENTATION

1. Ask students to name the letter in the box at the top of pupil page 18. Have them write it several times in their spiral notebooks on page 18.

2. Hold up the *radio* flash card and say *radio.* Emphasize the sound of the *R.* Ask the students to repeat several times. Point from the flash card to the picture on pupil page 18 while repeating the word. Ask the students to write the word in their spiral notebooks. Repeat with the other words on the page.

3. Ask students to raise their hands if their first or last names begin with the same sound heard in the words they just learned. Write those names on the *Rr* newsprint sheet. Ask if students know any other names that begin with the *R* sound. Ask them to write those names on the chalkboard. Help them with the spelling. Underline the beginning letter. If the names don't begin with *R,* let them write the names anyway and discover that they do not begin with the correct letter. Students can erase the names that don't belong. Names that begin with *R* can be added to the newsprint. Encourage students to keep adding names or words to the newsprint wall charts where words have already been written.

4. Ask students to choose one *R* word from the chart. This word will be their key word for remembering the sound represented by *R.* Have the students write this word in their spiral notebooks on page 18. Encourage the students to illustrate the object represented by their key word.

5. Direct the students' attention to the exercise at the bottom of pupil page 18. Explain that you will dictate a list of words. If the word begins with the *R* sound, they should circle the *Rr* beside the appropriate number. If the word does *not* begin with the *R* sound, students should mark an *X* over the *Rr.* Dictate: *1. lake 2. ran 3. ring 4. red 5. wing 6. load 7. led 8. wed 9. wake.*

Aa Bb Cc Dd Ee Ff Gg Hh Ii
Jj Kk Ll Mm Nn Oo Pp Qq **Rr**
Ss Tt Uu Vv Ww Xx Yy Zz

radio

rug

roof

rain

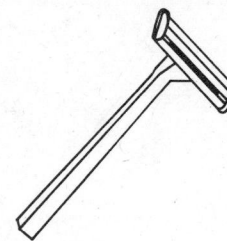

razor

record

1. R̶r̶   2. (Rr)   3. (Rr)
4. (Rr)   5. R̶r̶   6. R̶r̶
7. R̶r̶   8. R̶r̶   9. R̶r̶

Aa Bb Cc **Dd** Ee Ff Gg Hh Ii
Jj Kk Ll Mm Nn Oo Pp Qq Rr
Ss Tt Uu Vv Ww Xx Yy Zz

dog

door

dress

doctor

desk

dollar

1. (Dd)   2. ⨯⨯   3. (Dd)
4. (Dd)   5. ⨯⨯   6. ⨯⨯
7. ⨯⨯   8. (Dd)   9. ⨯⨯

19

OBJECTIVE

Students will associate the letter symbols Dd with the appropriate sound.

PREPARATION

Bring the alphabet flash cards. Prepare a set of flash cards containing the following words: *dog, door, dress, doctor, desk, dollar.*

PRESENTATION

1. Ask students to name the letter in the box at the top of pupil page 19. Have them write it several times in their spiral notebooks on page 19.

2. Hold up the *dog* flash card and say *dog*. Emphasize the sound of the *D*. Ask the students to repeat several times. Point from the flash card to the picture on pupil page 19 while repeating the word. Ask the students to write the word in their spiral notebooks. Repeat with the other words on the page.

3. Ask students to raise their hands if their first or last names begin with the same sound heard in the words they just learned. Write those names on the Dd newsprint sheet. Ask if students know any other names that begin with the *D* sound. Ask them to write those names on the chalkboard. Help them with the spelling. Underline the beginning letter. If the names don't begin with *D,* let them write the names anyway and discover that they do not begin with the correct letter. Students can erase the names that don't belong. Names that begin with *D* can be added to the newsprint. Encourage students to keep adding names or words to the newsprint wall charts where words have already been written.

4. Ask students to choose one *D* word from the chart. This word will be their key word for remembering the sound represented by *D*. Have the students write this word in their spiral notebooks on page 19. Encourage the students to illustrate the object represented by their key word.

5. Direct the students' attention to the exercise at the bottom of pupil page 19. Explain that you will dictate a list of words. If the word begins with the *D* sound, they should circle the *Dd* beside the appropriate number. If the word does *not* begin with the *D* sound, students should mark an *X* over the *Dd*. Dictate: *1. Dan 2. take 3. doughnut 4. date 5. tan 6. pill 7. fill 8. dad 9. pad.*

OBJECTIVE

Students will associate the letter symbols *Zz* with the appropriate sound.

PREPARATION

Bring the alphabet flash cards. Prepare a set of flash cards containing the following words: *zebra, zoo, zero, zip code, zipper, zigzag.*

PRESENTATION

1. Ask students to name the letter in the box at the top of pupil page 20. Have them write it several times in their spiral notebooks on page 20.

2. Hold up the *zebra* flash card and say *zebra*. Emphasize the sound of the Z. Ask the students to repeat several times. Point from the flash card to the picture on pupil page 20 while repeating the word. Ask the students to write the word in their spiral notebooks. Repeat with the other words on the page.

3. Ask students to raise their hands if their first or last names begin with the same sound heard in the words they just learned. Write those names on the *Zz* newsprint sheet. Ask if students know any other names that begin with the *Z* sound. Ask them to write those names on the chalkboard. Help them with the spelling. Underline the beginning letter. If the names don't begin with *Z*, let them write the names anyway and discover that they do not begin with the correct letter. Students can erase the names that don't belong. Names that begin with *Z* can be added to the newsprint. Encourage students to keep adding names or words to the newsprint wall charts where words have already been written.

4. Ask students to choose one *Z* word from the chart. This word will be their key word for remembering the sound represented by *Z*. Have the students write this word in their spiral notebooks on page 20. Encourage the students to illustrate the object represented by their key word.

5. Direct the students' attention to the exercise at the bottom of pupil page 20. Explain that you will dictate a list of words. If the word begins with the *Z* sound, they should circle the *Zz* beside the appropriate number. If the word does *not* begin with the *Z* sound, students should mark an *X* over the *Zz*. Dictate: *1. zinc 2. sing 3. sip 4. sink 5. zoom 6. sit 7. zing 8. zone 9. zest.*

Aa Bb Cc Dd Ee Ff Gg Hh Ii
Jj Kk Ll Mm Nn Oo Pp Qq Rr
Ss Tt Uu Vv Ww Xx Yy Zz

zebra

zoo

zero

Zip Code

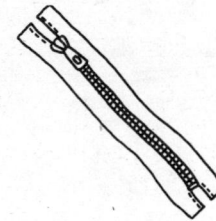

zipper

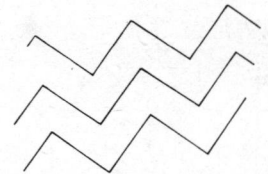

zig zag

1. (Zz) 2. (X̶Z̶z̶) 3. (X̶Z̶z̶)
4. (X̶Z̶z̶) 5. (Zz) 6. (X̶Z̶z̶)
7. (Zz) 8. (Zz) 9. (Zz)

__k__ey

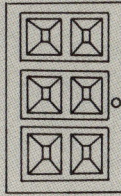

__d__oor

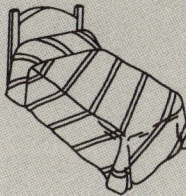

__b__ed

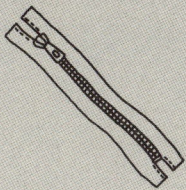

__z__ipper

__r__ain

__n__ickel

__b__us

__n__ose

__r__ug

1. ____Zz____   2. ____Nn____   3. ____Rr____

4. ____Nn____   5. ____Bb____   6. ____Dd____

7. ____Kk____   8. ____Dd____   9. ____Bb____

OBJECTIVE

Students will review the *Bb, Kk, Nn, Rr, Dd,* and, *Zz* sounds.

PREPARATION

Cut paper into strips for use in writing sentences.

PRESENTATION

1. Write *Bb, Kk, Nn, Rr, Dd,* and *Zz* on the chalkboard. Point to the letters one at a time. Ask the students to name each letter as you point.

2. Point to the illustrated key at the top of pupil page 21. Say *key.* Emphasize the beginning sound. Demonstrate filling in the appropriate letter on the blank line. Ask the students to complete the exercise in their texts.

3. On the blanks at the bottom of the page, have the students write the letter symbol for the sound they hear at the beginning of the following words: *1. zoom 2. new 3. raw 4. nine 5. ball 6. dim 7. Kelly 8. dirt 9. ball.* Have the students verify each other's responses.

4. Have the students create a Language Experience Story (LES) by following these steps:

   a. Write *book* on the chalkboard. Model the word and have students repeat. Ask individual students, *Where is your book? Tell me about your book.* As students respond to your questioning, write on the chalkboard, word for word, what each student dictates.

   b. Have everyone listen carefully as you read, several times, what the student has dictated. As you read, point to (track) each word.

   c. Now have all the students read the story on the board with you. Repeat this several times. Continue to point to (track) each word.

   d. Next, begin hesitating before certain words, waiting for the students to orally fill in the words that are being omitted.

   e. Now erase certain words in the story and, as you read, ask the students to orally supply the missing words. Fill in the blank spaces, as appropriate.

   f. Put the sentences of the student composition on sentence strips, one sentence per strip. Scramble the sentences. The students must put the sentences in correct order.

   g. Cut the strips into pieces, isolating individual words. Form several small groups of students. Distribute two or three sentence strips that have been cut into pieces to each group. Ask the groups to form new or original sentences from the cut-out words. Have the students write the dialogues in their spiral notebooks on page 21.

OBJECTIVE

Students will associate the letter symbols *Cc* with the appropriate sound.

PREPARATION

Create a set of picture flash cards for each group of four students by making enlarged photocopies of the illustrations on pupil page 22. Attach the photocopies to index cards.

PRESENTATION

1. Ask the students to name the letter in the box at the top of pupil page 22. Have them write the letter several times on page 22 of their spiral notebooks.

2. Write the words *coat, comb, cat, cup, car,* and *can* on the chalkboard. Point to the word *coat*. Pronounce it carefully and ask the students to repeat several times. Explain its meaning, using the students' native language if necessary. Repeat the process with the rest of the words.

3. Create groups of four students. Give each group a set of picture flash cards. As you dictate the words *coat, comb, cat, cup, car,* and *can*, have each group hold up the appropriate card. Have one member from each group attach a card to the appropriate newsprint chart.

4. Ask students to choose one *C* word from the chart. This word will be their key word for remembering the sound represented by *C*. Have the students write this word in their spiral notebooks on page 22. Encourage the students to illustrate the object represented by their key word.

5. Direct the students' attention to the exercise at the bottom of pupil page 22. Explain that you will dictate a list of words. If the word begins with the *C* sound, students should circle the Cc beside the appropriate number. If the word does *not* begin with the *C* sound, they should mark an *X* over the *Cc*. Dictate the following: *1. cake 2. gate 3. jack 4. cow 5. joke 6. calm 7. catch 8. goat 9. coat.*

Aa Bb [Cc] Dd Ee Ff Gg Hh Ii
Jj Kk Ll Mm Nn Oo Pp Qq Rr
Ss Tt Uu Vv Ww Xx Yy Zz

coat

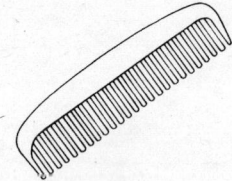
comb

cat

cup

car

can

1. (Cc)   2. ⊗   3. ⊗
4. (Cc)   5. ⊗   6. (Cc)
7. (Cc)   8. ⊗   9. (Cc)

22

Aa Bb Cc Dd Ee Ff Gg Hh Ii
Jj Kk Ll Mm Nn Oo Pp Qq Rr
Ss Tt Uu Vv Ww Xx Yy Zz

hat

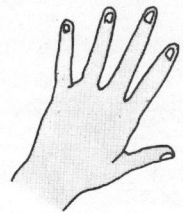
hand

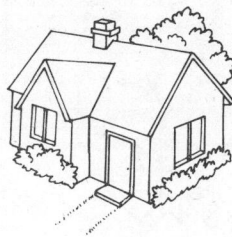
house

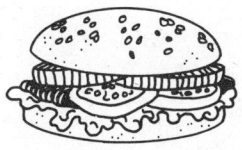
hamburger

hose

horse

1. X̶H̶h̶   2. X̶H̶h̶   3. (Hh)
4. X̶H̶h̶   5. (Hh)   6. X̶H̶h̶
7. (Hh)   8. X̶H̶h̶   9. (Hh)

23

OBJECTIVE

Students will associate the letter symbols *Hh* with the appropriate sound.

PREPARATION

Create a set of picture flash cards for each group of four students by making enlarged photocopies of the illustrations on pupil page 23. Attach the photocopies to index cards.

PRESENTATION

1. Ask the students to name the letter in the box at the top of pupil page 23. Have them write the letter several times on page 23 of their spiral notebooks.

2. Write the words *hat, hand, house, hamburger, hose,* and *horse,* on the chalkboard. Point to the word *hat.* Pronounce it carefully and ask the students to repeat several times. Explain its meaning, using the students' native language if necessary. Repeat the process with the rest of the words.

3. Create groups of four students. Give each group a set of picture flash cards. As you dictate the words *hat, hand, house, hamburger, hose,* and *horse,* have each group hold up the appropriate card. Have one member from each group attach a card to the appropriate newsprint chart.

4. Ask students to choose one *H* word from the chart. This word will be their key word for remembering the sound represented by *H.* Have the students write this word in their spiral notebooks on page 23. Encourage the students to illustrate the object represented by their key word.

5. Direct the students' attention to the exercise at the bottom of pupil page 23. Explain that you will dictate a list of words. If the word begins with the *H* sound, students should circle the *Hh* beside the appropriate number. If the word does *not* begin with the *H* sound, they should mark an *X* over the *Hh.* Dictate the following: *1. jug 2. van 3. hug 4. for 5. hog 6. fan 7. hand 8. ban 9. happy.*

OBJECTIVE

Students will associate the letter symbols *Vv* with the appropriate sound.

PREPARATION

Create a set of picture flash cards for each group of four students by making enlarged photocopies of the illustrations on pupil page 24. Attach the photocopies to index cards.

PRESENTATION

1. Ask the students to name the letter in the box at the top of pupil page 24. Have them write the letter several times on page 24 of their spiral notebooks.

2. Write the words *vest, van, vase, violin, vegetables,* and *vote* on the chalkboard. Point to the word *vest.* Pronounce it carefully and ask the students to repeat several times. Explain its meaning, using the students' native language if necessary. Repeat the process with the rest of the words.

3. Create groups of four students. Give each group a set of picture flash cards. As you dictate the words *vest, van, vase, violin, vegetables,* and *vote,* have each group hold up the appropriate card. Have one member from each group attach a card to the appropriate newsprint chart.

4. Ask students to choose one *V* word from the chart. This word will be their key word for remembering the sound represented by *V.* Have the students write this word in their spiral notebooks on page 24. Encourage the students to illustrate the object represented by their key word.

5. Direct the students' attention to the exercise at the bottom of pupil page 24. Explain that you will dictate a list of words. If the word begins with the *V* sound, students should circle the *Vv* beside the appropriate number. If the word does not begin with the *V* sound, they should mark an *X* over the *Vv.* Dictate the following: *1. visit 2. wine 3. boat 4. vet 5. wiper 6. wet 7. viper 8. vote 9. vine.*

Aa Bb Cc Dd Ee Ff Gg Hh Ii
Jj Kk Ll Mm Nn Oo Pp Qq Rr
Ss Tt Uu [Vv] Ww Xx Yy Zz

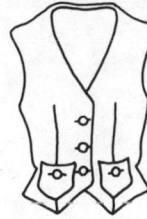

vest

van

vase

violin

vegetables

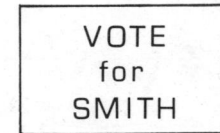

VOTE for SMITH

vote

1. (Vv) 2. X 3. X
4. (Vv) 5. X 6. X
7. (Vv) 8. (Vv) 9. (Vv)

24

24

Aa Bb Cc Dd Ee Ff Gg Hh Ii

J j Kk Ll Mm Nn Oo Pp Qq Rr

Ss Tt Uu Vv Ww Xx Yy Zz

jar

jacket

jeep

judge

jump

jet

1. J̶j̶   2. X̶X̶   3. Jj

4. Jj   5. X̶X̶   6. Jj

7. Jj   8. X̶X̶   9. Jj

OBJECTIVE

Students will associate the letter symbols *Jj* with the appropriate sound.

PREPARATION

Create a set of picture flash cards for each group of four students by making enlarged photocopies of the illustrations on pupil page 25. Attach the photocopies to index cards.

PRESENTATION

1. Ask the students to name the letter in the box at the top of pupil page 25. Have them write the letter several times on page 25 of their spiral notebooks.

2. Write the words *jar, jacket, jeep, judge, jump,* and *jet* on the chalkboard. Point to the word *jar*. Pronounce it carefully and ask the students to repeat several times. Explain its meaning, using the students' native language if necessary. Repeat the process with the rest of the words.

3. Create groups of four students. Give each group a set of picture flash cards. As you dictate the words *jar, jacket, jeep, judge, jump,* and *jet,* have each group hold up the appropriate card. Have one member from each group attach a card to the appropriate newsprint chart.

4. Ask students to choose one J word from the chart. This word will be their key word for remembering the sound represented by J. Have the students write this word in their spiral notebooks on page 25. Encourage the students to illustrate the object represented by their key word.

5. Direct the students' attention to the exercise at the bottom of pupil page 25. Explain that you will dictate a list of words. If the word begins with the *J* sound, students should circle the *Jj* beside the appropriate number. If the word does *not* begin with the *J* sound, they should mark an *X* over the *Jj*. Dictate the following: *1. hello 2. hail 3. jell 4. joke 5. Gail 6. job 7. Jane 8. hear 9. jump.*

OBJECTIVE

Students will associate the letter symbols *Gg* with the appropriate sound.

PREPARATION

Create a set of picture flash cards for each group of four students by making enlarged photocopies of the illustrations on pupil page 26. Attach the photocopies to index cards.

PRESENTATION

1. Ask the students to name the letter in the box at the top of pupil page 26. Have them write the letter several times on page 26 of their spiral notebooks.

2. Write the words *gas, gift, glass, grapes, gum,* and *gate* on the chalkboard. Point to the word *gas*. Pronounce it carefully and ask the students to repeat several times. Explain its meaning, using the students' native language if necessary. Repeat the process with the rest of the words.

3. Create groups of four students. Give each group a set of picture flash cards. As you dictate the words *gas, gift, glass, grapes, gum,* and *gate,* have each group hold up the appropriate card. Have one member from each group attach a card to the appropriate newsprint chart.

4. Ask students to choose one *G* word from the chart. This word will be their key word for remembering the sound represented by *G*. Have the students write this word in their spiral notebooks on page 26. Encourage the students to illustrate the object represented by their key word.

5. Direct the students' attention to the exercise at the bottom of pupil page 26. Explain that you will dictate a list of words. If the word begins with the *G* sound, students should circle the *Gg* beside the appropriate number. If the word does *not* begin with the *G* sound, they should mark an *X* over the *Gg*. Dictate the following: *1. get 2. kit 3. gun 4. knock 5. guard 6. gum 7. card 8. girl 9. curl.*

Aa Bb Cc Dd Ee Ff [Gg] Hh Ii
Jj Kk Ll Mm Nn Oo Pp Qq Rr
Ss Tt Uu Vv Ww Xx Yy Zz

gas

gift

glass

grapes

gum

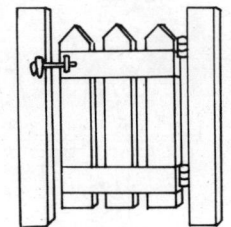

gate

1. (Gg) 2. ☒ 3. (Gg)
4. ☒ 5. (Gg) 6. (Gg)
7. ☒ 8. (Gg) 9. ☒

26

Aa Bb Cc Dd Ee Ff Gg Hh Ii
Jj Kk Ll Mm Nn Oo Pp Qq Rr
Ss Tt Uu Vv [Ww] Xx Yy Zz

window

well

wave

wasp

wood

watch

1. (Ww)　　2. (Ww)　　3. X̶W̶w̶

4. X̶W̶w̶　　5. (Ww)　　6. X̶W̶w̶

7. X̶W̶w̶　　8. (Ww)　　9. X̶W̶w̶

OBJECTIVE

Students will associate the letter symbols *Ww* with the appropriate sound.

PREPARATION

Create a set of picture flash cards for each group of four students by making enlarged photocopies of the illustrations on pupil page 27. Attach the photocopies to index cards.

PRESENTATION

1. Ask the students to name the letter in the box at the top of pupil page 27. Have them write the letter several times on page 27 of their spiral notebooks.

2. Write the words *window, well, wave, wasp, wood,* and *watch* on the chalkboard. Point to the word *window*. Pronounce it carefully and ask the students to repeat several times. Explain its meaning, using the students' native language if necessary. Repeat the process with the rest of the words.

3. Create groups of four students. Give each group a set of picture flash cards. As you dictate the words *window, well, wave, wasp, wood,* and *watch,* have each group hold up the appropriate card. Have one member from each group attach a card to the appropriate newsprint chart.

4. Ask students to choose one *W* word from the chart. This word will be their key word for remembering the sound represented by *W*. Have the students write this word in their spiral notebooks on page 27. Encourage the students to illustrate the object represented by their key word.

5. Direct the students' attention to the exercise at the bottom of pupil page 27. Explain that you will dictate a list of words. If the word begins with the *W* sound, students should circle the *Ww* beside the appropriate number. If the word does *not* begin with the *W* sound, they should mark an *X* over the *Ww*. Dictate the following: *1. wail 2. week 3. yell 4. vet 5. wet 6. veil 7. yet 8. west 9. vest.*

OBJECTIVE

Students will review associating the appropriate sounds for the following letter symbols: *Cc, Hh, Vv, Jj, Gg, Ww.*

PREPARATION

Cut paper into strips for use in writing sentences.

PRESENTATION

1. Write *Cc, Hh, Vv, Jj, Gg,* and *Ww* on the chalkboard. Point to the letters one at a time. Ask the students to name each letter as you point.

2. Point to the illustrated car at the top of pupil page 28. Say *car.* Emphasize the beginning sound. Demonstrate filling in the appropriate letter on the blank line. Ask the students to complete the exercise in their texts.

3. On the blanks at the bottom of the page, have the students write the letter symbol for the sound they hear at the beginning of the following words: *1. comb 2. veal 3. jam 4. holy 5. gain 6. widow 7. hotel 8. hope 9. game.*

4. Have the students create a Language Experience Story (LES) by following these steps:

   a. Write *car* on the chalkboard. Model the word and have the students repeat. Ask individual students, *Do you have a car? Tell me about it.* As students respond to your questioning, write on the chalkboard, word for word, what each student dictates.

   b. Have everyone listen carefully as you read, several times, what the student has dictated. As you read, point to (track) each word.

   c. Now have all the students read the story on the board with you. Repeat this several times. Continue to point to (track) each word.

   d. Next, begin hesitating before certain words, waiting for the students to orally fill in the words that are being omitted.

   e. Now erase certain words in the story and, as you read, ask the students to orally supply the missing words. Fill in the blank spaces, as appropriate.

   f. Put the sentences of the student composition on sentence strips, one sentence per strip. Scramble the sentences. The students must put the sentences in correct order.

   g. Cut the strips into pieces, isolating individual words. Form several small groups of students. Distribute two or three sentence strips that have been cut into pieces to each group. Ask the groups to form new or original sentences from the cut-out words. Have the students write the dialogues in their spiral notebooks on page 28.

  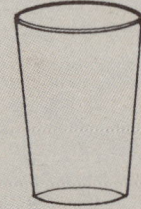

__*c*_ ar   __*v*_ est   __*g*_ lass

 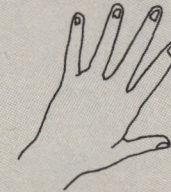 

__*w*_ indow   __*h*_ and   __*j*_ ump

 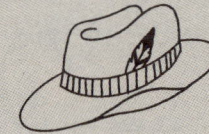 

__*c*_ up   __*h*_ at   __*g*_ rapes

1. ____*Cc*____   2. ____*Vv*____   3. ____*Jj*____

4. ____*Hh*____   5. ____*Gg*____   6. ____*Ww*____

7. ____*Hh*____   8. ____*Hh*____   9. ____*Gg*____

Aa Bb Cc Dd Ee Ff Gg Hh Ii
Jj Kk Ll Mm Nn Oo Pp Qq Rr
Ss Tt Uu Vv Ww Xx Yy Zz

yard

yarn

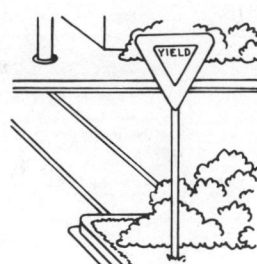

yield

yucca

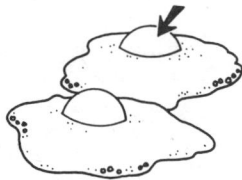

yolks

yawn

1. (Yy)   2. (Yy)   3. X̶
4. X̶   5. (Yy)   6. X̶
7. X̶   8. X̶   9. (Yy)

OBJECTIVE

Students will associate the letter symbols *Yy* with the appropriate sounds.

PREPARATION

Create a set of flash cards indicating the following words: *yard, yarn, yield, yucca, yolks,* and *yawn.*

PRESENTATION

1. Ask the students to name the letter in the box at the top of pupil page 29. Have them write the letter several times on page 29 of their spiral notebooks.

2. Write *yard, yarn, yield, yucca, yolks,* and *yawn* on the chalkboard. Point to the word *yard.* Pronounce it carefully and ask the students to repeat several times. Explain its meaning, using the students' native language if necessary. Have the students write the words in their spiral notebooks on page 29.

3. Create groups of four students. Give each group a set of flash cards. As you dictate *yard, yarn, yield, yucca, yolks,* and *yawn,* have each group hold up the appropriate card. Have one member from each group attach the card to the appropriate newsprint chart.

4. Ask students to choose one *Y* word from the chart. This word will be their key word for remembering the sound represented by *Y.* Have the students write this word in their spiral notebooks on page 29. Encourage the students to illustrate the object represented by their key word.

5. Direct the students' attention to the exercise at the bottom of pupil page 29. Explain that you will dictate a list of words. If the word begins with the *Y* sound, students should circle the *Yy* beside the appropriate number. If the word does *not* begin with the *Y* sound, students should mark an X over the *Yy.* Dictate: *1. yes 2. you 3. jar 4. west 5. yellow 6. jeer 7. wire 8. jell 9. year.*

OBJECTIVE

Students will associate the letter symbols *Qq* with the appropriate sound.

PREPARATION

Create a set of flash cards indicating the following words: *quarter, quail, quart, queen, question,* and *quilt*.

PRESENTATION

1. Ask the students to name the letter in the box at the top of pupil page 30. Have them write the letter several times on page 30 of their spiral notebooks.

2. Write *quarter, quail, quart, queen, question,* and *quilt* on the chalkboard. Pronounce each word carefully and ask the students to repeat them several times. Explain the words' meanings using the students' native language if necessary. Have the students write the words in their spiral notebooks on page 30.

3. Create groups of four students. Give each group a set of flash cards. As you dictate *quarter, quail, quart, queen, question,* and *quilt,* have each group hold up the appropriate card. Have one member from each group attach the card to the appropriate newsprint chart.

4. Ask students to choose one *Q* word from the chart. This word will be their key word for remembering the sound represented by *Q*. Have the students write this word in their spiral notebooks on page 30. Encourage the students to illustrate the object represented by their key word.

5. Direct the students' attention to the exercise at the bottom of pupil page 30. Explain that you will dictate a list of words. If the word begins with the *Q* sound, students should circle the *Qq* beside the appropriate number. If the word does *not* begin with the *Q* sound, students should mark an X over the *Qq*. Dictate: *1. quack 2. cake 3. quake 4. cart 5. quart 6. wart 7. your 8. queen 9. clean.*

Aa Bb Cc Dd Ee Ff Gg Hh Ii
Jj Kk Ll Mm Nn Oo Pp Qq Rr
Ss Tt Uu Vv Ww Xx Yy Zz

quarter

quail

quart

queen

question

quilt

1. (Qq)   2. ☒   3. (Qq)
4. ☒   5. (Qq)   6. ☒
7. ☒   8. (Qq)   9. ☒

30

Aa Bb Cc Dd Ee Ff Gg Hh Ii
Jj Kk Ll Mm Nn Oo Pp Qq Rr
Ss Tt Uu Vv Ww ⊡Xx Yy Zz

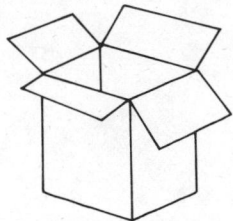

box

six

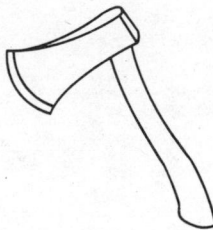

ax

fox

wax

ox

1. (Xx) 2. ☒ 3. ☒

4. (Xx) 5. (Xx) 6. ☒

7. (Xx) 8. (Xx) 9. ☒

31

OBJECTIVE

Students will associate the letter symbols *Xx* with the appropriate sound.

PREPARATION

Create a set of flash cards indicating the following words: *box, six, ax, fox, wax,* and *ox.*

PRESENTATION

1. Ask the students to name the letter in the box at the top of pupil page 31. Have them write the letter several times on page 31 of their spiral notebooks.

2. Write *box, six, ax, fox, wax,* and *ox* on the chalkboard. Pronounce each word carefully and ask the students to repeat them several times. Explain the words' meanings using the students' native language if necessary. Have the students write the words in their spiral notebooks on page 31.

3. Create groups of four students. Give each group a set of flash cards. As you dictate *box, six, ax, fox, wax, and ox,* have each group hold up the appropriate card. Have one member from each group attach the card to the appropriate newsprint chart.

4. Ask students to choose one *X* word from the chart. This word will be their key word for remembering the sound represented by *X*. Have the students write this word in their spiral notebooks on page 31. Encourage the students to illustrate the object represented by their key word.

5. Direct the students' attention to the exercise at the bottom of pupil page 31. Explain that you will dictate a list of words. If the word begins with the *X* sound, students should circle the *Xx* beside the appropriate number. If the word does *not* begin with the *X* sound, students should mark an *X* over the *Xx*. Dictate: *1. lax 2. seep 3. oyster 4. Xerox 5. lox 6. salt 7. mix 8. fix 9. fizz.*

OBJECTIVE

Students will review associating the letter symbols *Qq and Yy* with the appropriate sounds, and review the ending sound of *Xx.*

PREPARATION

Cut paper into strips for use in writing sentences.

PRESENTATION

1. Write *Qq, Yy,* and *Xx* on the chalkboard. Point to the letters one at a time. Ask the students to name each letter as you point.

2. Point to the illustrations at the top of pupil page 32. Say *yard.* Emphasize the beginning sound. Demonstrate filling in the appropriate letter on the blank line. Ask the students to complete the exercise in their texts.

3. On the blanks at the bottom of the page, have the students write the letter symbol for the *Q, Y,* and *X* sounds that they hear in the following words: *1. yell 2. quick 3. quail 4. yellow 5. tax 6. yearn* 7. *fix 8. quiet 9. wax.*

4. Have the students create a Language Experience Story (LES) by following these steps:

   a. Write *quart* on the chalkboard. Ask individual students, *Do you buy milk by the quart?* As students respond to your questioning, write on the chalkboard, word for word, what each student dictates.

   b. Have everyone listen carefully as you read, several times, what the student has dictated. As you read, point to (track) each word.

   c. Now have all the students read the story on the board with you. Repeat this several times. Continue to point to (track) each word.

   d. Next, begin hesitating before certain words, waiting for the students to orally fill in the words that are being omitted.

   e. Now erase certain words in the story and, as you read, ask the students to orally supply the missing words. Fill in the blank spaces, as appropriate.

   f. Put the sentences of the student composition on sentence strips, one sentence per strip. Scramble the sentences. The students must put the sentences in correct order.

   g. Cut the strips into pieces, isolating individual words. Form several small groups of students. Distribute two or three sentence strips that have been cut into pieces to each group. Ask the groups to form new or original sentences from the cut-out words. Have the students write the dialogues in their spiral notebooks on page 32.

  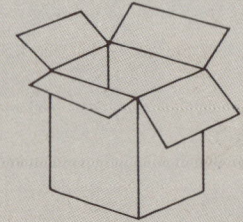

__*y*__ard   __*q*__uarter   bo__*x*__

__*y*__arn   si__*x*__   __*q*__uail

 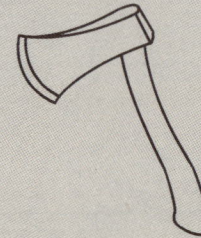 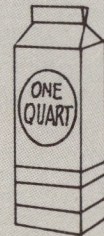

__*y*__ucca   a__*x*__   __*q*__uart

1. ____*Yy*____   2. ____*Qq*____   3. ____*Qq*____

4. ____*Yy*____   5. ____*Xx*____   6. ____*Yy*____

7. ____*Xx*____   8. ____*Qq*____   9. ____*Xx*____

1. _____ Mm _____	2. _____ Ss _____	3. _____ Tt _____
4. _____ Pp _____	5. _____ Jj _____	6. _____ Ff _____
7. _____ Cc _____	8. _____ Hh _____	9. _____ Kk _____
10. _____ Rr _____	11. _____ Rr _____	12. _____ Vv _____

_m_oney

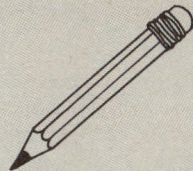

_p_encil

_f_ire

_r_ug

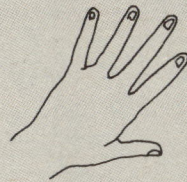

_h_and

_d_og

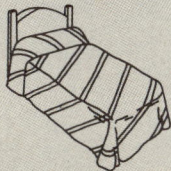

_b_ed

_k_itten

_n_ose

33

OBJECTIVE

Students will review the sound symbol association of beginning consonants.

PREPARATION

Cut paper into strips for use in writing sentences.

PRESENTATION

1. Write all beginning consonants (uppercase and lowercase) on the chalkboard. Point to the letters one at a time. Ask the students to name each letter as you point.

2. On the blanks at the top of the page, have the students write the letter symbol for the sound they hear at the beginning of the following words: _1. ail 2. sip 3.time 4. pig 5. jam 6. feel 7. call 8. hug 9. keep 10. ring 11. rotten 12. vet._

3. Point to the illustrations on pupil page 33. Emphasize the beginning sound of each. Demonstrate filling in the appropriate letter on the blank line. Ask the students to fill in the appropriate letters in their texts.

4. Have the students create a Language Experience Story (LES) by following these steps:

a. Write the words _kitten_ and _cat_ on the chalkboard. Model the words. Have the students repeat. Ask individual students, _Do you have a kitten? Do you have a cat? Tell me about them._ As students respond to your questioning, write on the chalkboard, word for word, what each student dictates.

b. Have everyone listen carefully as you read, several times, what the student has dictated. As you read, point to (track) each word.

c. Now have all the students read the story on the board with you. Repeat this several times. Continue to point to (track) each word.

d. Next, begin hesitating before certain words, waiting for the students to orally fill in the words that are being omitted.

e. Now erase certain words in the story and, as you read, ask the students to orally supply the missing words. Fill in the blank spaces, as appropriate.

f. Put the sentences of the student composition on sentence strips, one sentence per strip. Scramble the sentences. The students must put the sentences in correct order.

g. Cut the strips into pieces, isolating individual words. Form several small groups of students. Distribute two or three sentence strips that have been cut into pieces to each group. Ask the groups to form new or original sentences from the cut-out words. Have the students write the dialogues in their spiral notebooks on page 33.

OBJECTIVE

Students will associate the letter symbols *Aa* with the appropriate short sounds.

PREPARATION

Create a set of flash cards indicating the following words: *ant, apple, fan, man, lamp, hat.*

PRESENTATION

1. Ask the students to name the letter in the box at the top of pupil page 34. Have them write the letter several times on page 34 of their spiral notebooks.

2. Write *ant, apple, fan, man, lamp,* and *hat* on the chalkboard. Pronounce the words carefully and ask the students to repeat several times. If necessary, use the students' native language to explain any new vocabulary. Have the students write the words in their spiral notebooks on page 34.

3. Create groups of four students. Give each group a set of flash cards. As you dictate *ant, apple, fan, man, lamp,* and *hat,* have each group hold up the appropriate card. Have one member from each group attach the card to the appropriate newsprint chart.

4. Ask students to choose one *A* word from the chart. This word will be their key word for remembering the sound represented by *A.* Have the students write this word in their spiral notebooks on page 34. Encourage the students to illustrate the object represented by their key word.

5. Direct the students' attention to the exercise at the bottom of pupil page 34. Explain that you will dictate a list of words. If the word contains the short *A* sound, students should circle the *Aa* beside the appropriate number. If the word does *not* contain the short *A* sound, students should mark an *X* over the *Aa.* Dictate: *1. and 2. gas 3. book 4. fight 5. happy 6. dance 7. check 8. cat 9. bad.*

Aa Bb Cc Dd Ee Ff Gg Hh Ii
Jj Kk Ll Mm Nn Oo Pp Qq Rr
Ss Tt Uu Vv Ww Xx Yy Zz

ant

apple

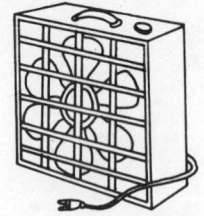

fan

man

lamp

hat

1. (Aa) 2. (Aa) 3. (A̶a̶)

4. (A̶a̶) 5. (Aa) 6. (Aa)

7. (A̶a̶) 8. (Aa) 9. (Aa)

34

Aa Bb Cc Dd Ee Ff Gg Hh Ii
Jj Kk Ll Mm Nn Oo Pp Qq Rr
Ss Tt Uu Vv Ww Xx Yy Zz

egg

bench

web

bed

belt

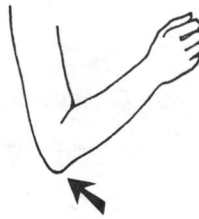

elbow

1. (Ee)   2. ~~Ee~~   3. (Ee)

4. (Ee)   5. (Ee)   6. ~~Ee~~

7. (Ee)   8. ~~Ee~~   9. (Ee)

35

OBJECTIVE

Students will associate the letter symbols *Ee* with the appropriate short sound.

PREPARATION

Create a set of flash cards indicating the following words: *egg, bench, web, bed, belt,* and *elbow.*

PRESENTATION

1. Ask the students to name the letter in the box at the top of pupil page 35. Have them write the letter several times on page 35 of their spiral notebooks.

2. Write *egg, bench, web, bed, belt,* and *elbow* on the chalkboard. Pronounce the words carefully and ask the students to repeat several times. If necessary, use the students' native language to explain any new vocabulary. Emphasize the vowel sound. Have the students write the words in their spiral notebooks on page 35.

3. Create groups of four students. Give each group a set of flash cards. As you dictate *egg, bench, web, bed, belt,* and *elbow,* have each group hold up the appropriate card. Have one member from each group attach the card to the appropriate newsprint chart.

4. Ask students to choose one *E* word from the chart. This word will be their key word for remembering the sound represented by *E*. Have the students write this word in their spiral notebooks on page 35. Encourage the students to illustrate the object represented by their key word.

5. Direct the students' attention to the exercise at the bottom of pupil page 35. Explain that you will dictate a list of words. If the word contains the *E* sound, students should circle the *Ee* beside the appropriate number. If the word does *not* contain the *E* sound, students should mark an *X* over the *Ee*. Dictate: *1. head 2. run 3. elm 4. ten 5. rent 6. house 7. edge 8. dirt 9. end.*

OBJECTIVE

Students will associate the letter symbols *Ii* with the appropriate short sound.

PREPARATION

Create a set of flash cards indicating the following words: *ink, inch, milk, fish, six,* and *sink.*

PRESENTATION

1. Ask the students to name the letter in the box at the top of pupil page 36. Have them write the letter several times on page 36 of their spiral notebooks.

2. Write *ink, inch, milk, fish, six,* and *sink* on the chalkboard. Pronounce the words carefully and ask the students to repeat several times. If necessary, use the students' native language to explain any new vocabulary. Emphasize the vowel sound. Have the students write the words in their spiral notebooks on page 36.

3. Create groups of four students. Give each group a set of flash cards. As you dictate *ink, inch, milk, fish, six,* and *sink,* have each group hold up the appropriate card. Have one member from each group attach the card to the appropriate newsprint chart.

4. Ask students to choose one *I* word from the chart. This word will be their key word for remembering the sound represented by *I*. Have the students write this word in their spiral notebooks on page 36. Encourage the students to illustrate the object represented by their key word.

5. Direct the students' attention to the exercise at the bottom of pupil page 36. Explain that you will dictate a list of words. If the word contains the *I* sound, students should circle the *Ii* beside the appropriate number. If the word does *not* contain the *I* sound, students should mark an *X* over the *Ii*. Dictate: *1. drink 2. gum 3. it 4. lid 5. sand 6. ball 7. hit 8. pin 9. if.*

Aa Bb Cc Dd Ee Ff Gg Hh Ii
Jj Kk Ll Mm Nn Oo Pp Qq Rr
Ss Tt Uu Vv Ww Xx Yy Zz

ink

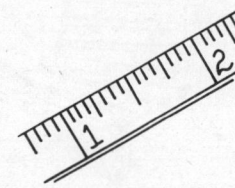

inch

milk

fish

six

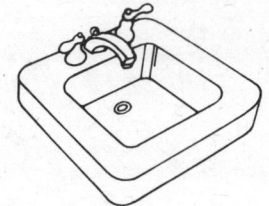

sink

1. (Ii) 2. X 3. (Ii)
4. (Ii) 5. X 6. X
7. (Ii) 8. (Ii) 9. (Ii)

Aa Bb Cc Dd Ee Ff Gg Hh Ii
Jj Kk Ll Mm Nn Oo Pp Qq Rr
Ss Tt Uu Vv Ww Xx Yy Zz

octopus

pot

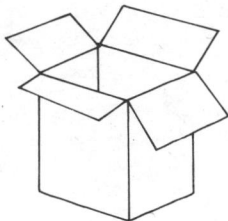

box

rock

mop

fox

1. (Oo)   2. ⊗   3. ⊗

4. (Oo)   5. (Oo)   6. (Oo)

7. (Oo)   8. (Oo)   9. ⊗

OBJECTIVE

Students will associate the letter symbols *Oo* with the appropriate short sound.

PREPARATION

Create a set of flash cards indicating the following words: *octopus, pot, box, rock, mop,* and *fox.*

PRESENTATION

1. Ask the students to name the letter in the box at the top of pupil page 37. Have them write the letter several times on page 37 of their spiral notebooks.

2. Write *octopus, pot, box, rock, mop,* and *fox* on the chalkboard. Pronounce the words carefully and ask the students to repeat several times. If necessary, use the students' native language to explain any new vocabulary. Emphasize the vowel sound. Have the students write the words in their spiral notebooks on page 37.

3. Create groups of four students. Give each group a set of flash cards. As you dictate *octopus, pot, box, rock, mop,* and *fox,* have each group hold up the appropriate card. Have one member from each group attach the card to the appropriate newsprint chart.

4. Ask students to choose one *O* word from the chart. This word will be their key word for remembering the sound represented by *O.* Have the students write this word in their spiral notebooks on page 37. Encourage the students to illustrate the object represented by their key word.

5. Direct the students' attention to the exercise at the bottom of pupil page 37. Explain that you will dictate a list of words. If the word contains the *O* sound, students should circle the *Oo* beside the appropriate number. If the word does *not* contain the *O* sound, students should mark an *X* over the *Oo.* Dictate: *1. pop 2. said 3. cup 4. stop 5. got 6. not 7. pond 8. stop 9. bag.*

OBJECTIVE

Students will associate the letter symbols *Uu* with the appropriate short sound.

PREPARATION

Create a set of flash cards indicating the following words: *up, duck, cup, bus, rug,* and *sun.*

PRESENTATION

1. Ask the students to name the letter in the box at the top of pupil page 38. Have them write the letter several times on page 38 of their spiral notebooks.

2. Write *up, duck, cup, bus, rug,* and *sun* on the chalkboard. Pronounce the words carefully and ask the students to repeat several times. If necessary, use the students' native language to explain any new vocabulary. Emphasize the vowel sound. Have the students write the words in their spiral notebooks on page 38.

3. Create groups of four students. Give each group a set of flash cards. As you dictate *up, duck, cup, bus, rug,* and *sun,* have each group hold up the appropriate card. Have one member from each group attach the card to the appropriate newsprint chart.

4. Ask students to choose one *U* word from the chart. This word will be their key word for remembering the sound represented by *U.* Have the students write this word in their spiral notebooks on page 38. Encourage the students to illustrate the object represented by their key word.

5. Direct the students' attention to the exercise at the bottom of pupil page 38. Explain that you will dictate a list of words. If the word contains the *U* sound, students should circle the *Uu* beside the appropriate number. If the word does *not* contain the *U* sound, students should mark an X over the *Uu.* Dictate: *1. tub 2. dad 3. mud 4. fun 5. rain 6. cup 7. us 8. up 9. match.*

Aa Bb Cc Dd Ee Ff Gg Hh Ii
Jj Kk Ll Mm Nn Oo Pp Qq Rr
Ss Tt [Uu] Vv Ww Xx Yy Zz

up

duck

cup

bus

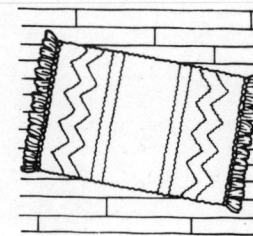

rug

sun

1. (Uu)   2. ☒   3. (Uu)

4. (Uu)   5. ☒   6. (Uu)

7. (Uu)   8. (Uu)   9. ☒

38

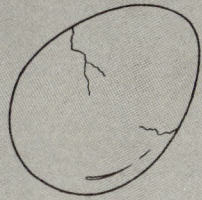

__e__ gg

m __i__ lk

c __u__ p

f __o__ x

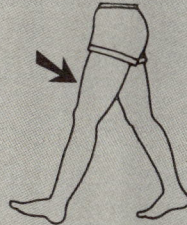

l __e__ g

f __a__ n

b __u__ s

__i__ nk

h __a__ t

1. _____*Oo*_____   2. _____*Aa*_____   3. _____*Ee*_____

4. _____*Ii*_____   5. _____*Aa*_____   6. _____*Ii*_____

7. _____*Ee*_____   8. _____*Uu*_____   9. _____*Oo*_____

39

OBJECTIVE

Students will review short vowel sounds.

PREPARATION

Cut paper into strips for use in writing sentences.

PRESENTATION

1. Write the vowels on the chalkboard. Point to the letters one at a time. Ask the students to name each letter as you point.

2. Point to the egg at the top of pupil page 39. Say *egg*. Emphasize the vowel sound. Demonstrate filling in the appropriate letter on the blank line. Ask the students to complete the exercise in their texts.

3. On the blanks at the bottom of the page, have the students write the letter symbol for the vowel sound they hear in the following words: *1. dot 2. catch 3. spell 4. is 5. am 6. rich 7. next 8. luck 9. rod.* Have the students verify each other's responses.

4. Have the students create a Language Experience Story (LES) by following these steps:

   a. Write *egg* on the chalkboard. Model the word. Have students repeat. Ask individual students, *Where do you buy eggs?* or *Do you like eggs?* or *Are eggs good for you?* As students respond to your questioning, write on the chalkboard, word for word, what each student dictates.

   b. Have everyone listen carefully as you read, several times, what the student has dictated. As you read, point to (track) each word.

   c. Now have all the students read the story on the board with you. Repeat this several times. Continue to point to (track) each word.

   d. Next, begin hesitating before certain words, waiting for the students to orally fill in the words that are being omitted.

   e. Now erase certain words in the story and, as you read, ask the students to orally supply the missing words. Fill in the blank spaces, as appropriate.

   f. Put the sentences of the student composition on sentence strips, one sentence per strip. Scramble the sentences. The students must put the sentences in correct order.

   g. Cut the strips into pieces, isolating individual words. Form several small groups of students. Distribute two or three sentence strips that have been cut into pieces to each group. Ask the groups to form new or original sentences from the cut-out words. Have the students write the dialogues in their spiral notebooks on page 39.

OBJECTIVE

Students will review short vowel sounds.

PREPARATION

Cut paper into strips for use in writing sentences.

PRESENTATION

1. Direct the students' attention to the exercise at the top of pupil page 40. Explain that you will dictate a list of words. Have students circle the uppercase and lowercase letter of the vowel sound if they hear it in the dictated word. If not, they should mark an *X* over the letters. Dictate: *1. bat 2. fix 3. shop 4. odd 5. boat 6. snake 7. get 8. fuzz 9. nut.*

2. In the middle of pupil page 40, have students write the uppercase and lowercase letter of the vowel sound they hear for each word. Dictate: *1. rag 2. etch 3. send 4. is 5. duck 6. sock 7. hot 8. dad 9. run.*

3. Point to the first illustration at the bottom of pupil page 40. Say *watch*. Demonstrate writing the appropriate vowel sound on the blank line. Ask students to do the same in their texts. Do the same with the remaining illustrations.

4. Ask the students to write the alphabet in their spiral notebooks on page 40.

5. Have the students create a Language Experience Story (LES) by following these steps:

a. Write *bus* on the chalkboard. Model the word. Have students repeat. Ask individual students, *Do you ride the bus? Where do you go? Tell me about it.* As students respond to your questioning, write on the chalkboard, word for word, what each student dictates.

b. Have everyone listen carefully as you read, several times, what the student has dictated. As you read, point to (track) each word.

c. Now have all the students read the story on the board with you. Repeat this several times. Continue to point to (track) each word.

d. Next, begin hesitating before certain words, waiting for the students to orally fill in the words that are being omitted.

e. Now erase certain words in the story and, as you read, ask the students to orally supply the missing words. Fill in the blank spaces, as appropriate.

f. Put the sentences of the student composition on sentence strips, one sentence per strip. Scramble the sentences. The students must put the sentences in correct order.

g. Cut the strips into pieces, isolating individual words. Form several small groups of students. Distribute two or three sentence strips that have been cut into pieces to each group. Ask the groups to form new or original sentences from the cut-out words. Have the students write the dialogues in their spiral notebooks on page 40.

1. (Aa)   2. (Ii)   3. (Oo)
4. (Oo)   5. ~~Aa~~   6. ~~Ee~~
7. (Ee)   8. (Uu)   9. ~~Ii~~

1. _____ *Aa*   2. _____ *Ee*   3. _____ *Ee*
4. _____ *Ii*   5. _____ *Uu*   6. _____ *Oo*
7. _____ *Oo*   8. _____ *Aa*   9. _____ *Uu*

1. w_*a*_tch   2. b_*e*_lt   3. b_*u*_s

4. s_*o*_ck   5. r_*i*_ng   6. sh_*e*_ll

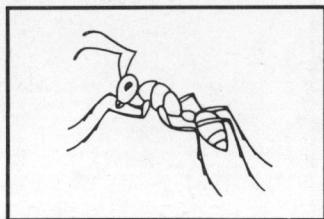

ant

ape

1. **apple**

   ~~ant~~ ape

2. **fan**

   ~~ant~~ ape

3. **snake**

   ant ~~ape~~

4. **rake**

   ant ~~ape~~

5. **hat**

   ~~ant~~ ape

6. **lamp**

   ~~ant~~ ape

7. **hand**

   ~~ant~~ ape

8. **man**

   ~~ant~~ ape

9. **gate**

   ant ~~ape~~

OBJECTIVE

Students will differentiate the short and long *A* sounds.

PREPARATION

Make photocopied enlargements of the ant and ape at the top of pupil page 41. Attach the illustrations on opposite sides of the chalkboard.

PRESENTATION

1. Point to the ant at the top of pupil page 41 and then to the ant on the chalkboard. Say *ant* several times. Emphasize the sound of the *Aa*. Do the same with *ape*.

2. Point to illustration #1 on pupil page 41. Say *apple* with an emphasis on the *A* sound. Ask the students whether the *A* in *apple* sounds like the *A* in *ant*. Does it sound like the *A* in *ape*? Model circling the correct response under the illustration. Ask the students to do the same in their texts. Repeat with the remaining illustrations.

3. Have the students create a Language Experience Story (LES) by following these steps:

   a. Write *plane* on the chalkboard. Model the word. Have students repeat. Ask individual students, *Have you been on a plane? Where did you go? Tell me about it.* As students respond to your questioning, write on the chalkboard, word for word, what each student dictates.

   b. Have everyone listen carefully as you read, several times, what the student has dictated. As you read, point to (track) each word.

   c. Now have all the students read the story on the board with you. Repeat this several times. Continue to point to (track) each word.

   d. Next, begin hesitating before certain words, waiting for the students to orally fill in the words that are being omitted.

   e. Now erase certain words in the story and, as you read, ask the students to orally supply the missing words. Fill in the blank spaces, as appropriate.

   f. Put the sentences of the student composition on sentence strips, one sentence per strip. Scramble the sentences. The students must put the sentences in correct order.

   g. Cut the strips into pieces, isolating individual words. Form several small groups of students. Distribute two or three sentence strips that have been cut into pieces to each group. Ask the groups to form new or original sentences from the cut-out words. Have the students write the dialogues in their spiral notebooks on page 41.

OBJECTIVE

Students will differentiate the short and long *E* sounds.

PREPARATION

Make photocopied enlargements of the illustrations at the top of pupil page 42. Attach the illustrations to opposite sides of the chalkboard.

PRESENTATION

1. Point to the egg at the top of pupil page 42 and then to the egg on the chalkboard. Say *egg* several times. Emphasize the sound of the *E*. Do the same with *eat*.

2. Point to illustration #1 on pupil page 41. Say *tree* with an emphasis on the *E* sound. Ask the students whether the *E* in *tree* sounds like the *E* in *egg*. Does it sound like the *E* in *eat*? Model circling the correct response under the illustration. Ask the students to do the same in their texts. Repeat with the remaining illustrations.

3. Have the students create a Language Experience Story (LES) by following these steps:

   a. Write *eat* or *key* on the chalkboard. Model the words. Have the students repeat. Ask individual students, *Where do like to eat, at home or in a restaurant? Why?* or *How many keys do you have? What are the keys for?* As students respond to your questioning, write on the chalkboard, word for word, what each student dictates.

   b. Have everyone listen carefully as you read, several times, what the student has dictated. As you read, point to (track) each word.

   c. Now have all the students read the story on the board with you. Repeat this several times. Continue to point to (track) each word.

   d. Next, begin hesitating before certain words, waiting for the students to orally fill in the words that are being omitted.

   e. Now erase certain words in the story and, as you read, ask the students to orally supply the missing words. Fill in the blank spaces, as appropriate.

   f. Put the sentences of the student composition on sentence strips, one sentence per strip. Scramble the sentences. The students must put the sentences in correct order.

   g. Cut the strips into pieces, isolating individual words. Form several small groups of students. Distribute two or three sentence strips that have been cut into pieces to each group. Ask the groups to form new or original sentences from the cut-out words. Have the students write the dialogues in their spiral notebooks on page 42.

egg

eat

1. *tree*

egg (eat)

2. *bee*

egg (eat)

3. *dress*

(egg) eat

4. *bed*

(egg) eat

5. *leaf*

egg (eat)

6. *key*

egg (eat)

7. *leg*

(egg) eat

8. *net*

(egg) eat

9. *teeth*
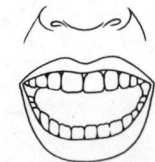
egg (eat)

42

ink

ice

1. **fire**

ink (ice)

2. **bike**

ink (ice)

3. **fish**

(ink) ice

4. **milk**

(ink) ice

5. **nine**

ink (ice)

6. **pig**

(ink) ice

7. **sink**

(ink) ice

8. **tire**

ink (ice)

9. **dime**

ink (ice)

43

OBJECTIVE

Students will differentiate the short and long *I* sounds.

PREPARATION

Make photocopied enlargements of the illustrations at the top of pupil page 43. Attach the illustrations to opposite sides of the chalkboard.

PRESENTATION

1. Point to the ink at the top of pupil page 43 and then to the ink on the chalkboard. Say *ink* several times. Emphasize the sound of the *I*. Do the same with *ice*.

2. Point to illustration #1 on pupil page 43. Say *fire* with an emphasis on the *I* sound. Ask the students whether the *I* in *fire* sounds like the *I* in *ink*. Does it sound like the *I* in *ice*? Model circling the correct response under the illustration. Ask the students to do the same in their texts. Repeat with the remaining illustrations.

3. Have the students create a Language Experience Story (LES) by following these steps:

a. Model *bike* or *fish* on the chalkboard. Model the words. Have the students repeat. Ask individual students, *Do you have a bike? Where do you ride?* or *Do you eat fish? What kind of fish?* As students respond to your questioning, write on the chalkboard, word for word, what each student dictates.

b. Have everyone listen carefully as you read, several times, what the student has dictated. As you read, point to (track) each word.

c. Now have all the students read the story on the board with you. Repeat this several times. Continue to point to (track) each word.

d. Next, begin hesitating before certain words, waiting for the students to orally fill in the words that are being omitted.

e. Now erase certain words in the story and, as you read, ask the students to orally supply the missing words. Fill in the blank spaces, as appropriate.

f. Put the sentences of the student composition on sentence strips, one sentence per strip. Scramble the sentences. The students must put the sentences in correct order.

g. Cut the strips into pieces, isolating individual words. Form several small groups of students. Distribute two or three sentence strips that have been cut into pieces to each group. Ask the groups to form new or original sentences from the cut-out words. Have the students write the dialogues in their spiral notebooks on page 43.

OBJECTIVE

Students will differentiate the short and long *O* sounds.

PREPARATION

Make photocopied enlargements of the illustrations at the top of pupil page 44. Attach the illustrations to opposite sides of the chalkboard.

PRESENTATION

1. Point to the octopus at the top of pupil page 44 and then to the octopus on the chalkboard. Say *octopus* several times. Emphasize the sound of the *O*. Do the same with *ocean*.

2. Point to illustration #1 on pupil page 44. Say *mop* with an emphasis on the *O* sound. Ask the students whether the *O* in *mop* sounds like the *O* in *octopus*. Does it sound like the *O* in *ocean*? Model circling the correct response under the illustration. Ask the students to do the same in their texts. Repeat with the remaining illustrations.

3. Have the students create a Language Experience Story (LES) by following these steps:

   a. Write *ocean* on the chalkboard. Model the word. Have the students repeat. Ask individual students, *Is there an ocean near your (native) country? What is the name of this ocean? Did you swim in this ocean?* As students respond to your questioning, write on the chalkboard, word for word, what each student dictates.

   b. Have everyone listen carefully as you read, several times, what the student has dictated. As you read, point to (track) each word.

   c. Now have all the students read the story on the board with you. Repeat this several times. Continue to point to (track) each word.

   d. Next, begin hesitating before certain words, waiting for the students to orally fill in the words that are being omitted.

   e. Now erase certain words in the story and, as you read, ask the students to orally supply the missing words. Fill in the blank spaces, as appropriate.

   f. Put the sentences of the student composition on sentence strips, one sentence per strip. Scramble the sentences. The students must put the sentences in correct order.

   g. Cut the strips into pieces, isolating individual words. Form several small groups of students. Distribute two or three sentence strips that have been cut into pieces to each group. Ask the groups to form new or original sentences from the cut-out words. Have the students write the dialogues in their spiral notebooks on page 44.

octopus

ocean

1. **mop**

(octopus)   ocean

2. **cot**

(octopus)   ocean

3. **stove**

octopus   (ocean)

4. **goat**

octopus   (ocean)

5. **pot**

(octopus)   ocean

6. **nose**

octopus   (ocean)

7. **fox**

(octopus)   ocean

8. **boat**

octopus   (ocean)

9. **sock**

(octopus)   ocean

44

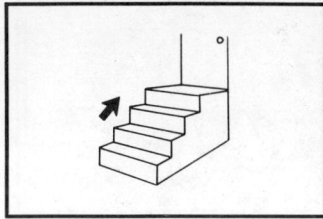

1. *mule* up · (United States)	2. *cup* (up) · United States	3. *gum* (up) · United States
4. *rug* (up) · United States	5. *bus* (up) · United States	6. *sun* (up) · United States
7. *bathtub* (up) · United States	8. *suit* up · (United States)	9. *umbrella* (up) · United States

up

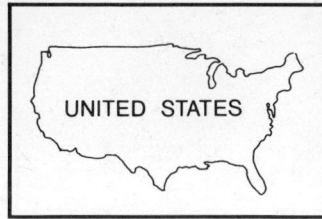

United States

OBJECTIVE

Students will differentiate the short and long *U* sounds.

PREPARATION

Make photocopied enlargements of the illustrations at the top of pupil page 45. Attach the illustrations to opposite sides of the chalkboard.

PRESENTATION

1. Point to the stairs at the top of pupil page 45 and then to the stairs on the chalkboard. Say *up* several times. Emphasize the sound of the *U*. Do the same with *United States*.

2. Point to illustration #1 on pupil page 45. Say *mule* with an emphasis on the *U* sound. Ask the students whether the *U* in *mule* sounds like the *U* in *up*. Does it sound like the *U* in *United States*? Model circling the correct response under the illustration. Ask the students to do the same in their texts. Repeat with the remaining illustrations.

3. Have the students create a Language Experience Story (LES) by following these steps:

   a. Write *United States* on the chalkboard. Model the words. Have the students repeat. Ask individual students, *Where is the United States? Is it near Mexico? Is it near your native country?* As students respond to your questioning, write on the chalkboard, word for word, what each student dictates.

   b. Have everyone listen carefully as you read, several times, what the student has dictated. As you read, point to (track) each word.

   c. Now have all the students read the story on the board with you. Repeat this several times. Continue to point to (track) each word.

   d. Next, begin hesitating before certain words, waiting for the students to orally fill in the words that are being omitted.

   e. Now erase certain words in the story and, as you read, ask the students to orally supply the missing words. Fill in the blank spaces, as appropriate.

   f. Put the sentences of the student composition on sentence strips, one sentence per strip. Scramble the sentences. The students must put the sentences in correct order.

   g. Cut the strips into pieces, isolating individual words. Form several small groups of students. Distribute two or three sentence strips that have been cut into pieces to each group. Ask the groups to form new or original sentences from the cut-out words. Have the students write the dialogues in their spiral notebooks on page 45.

OBJECTIVE

Students will differentiate between the sounds of *Y* in *yarn* and *baby*.

PREPARATION

Make photocopied enlargements of the illustrations at the top of pupil page 46. Attach the illustrations to opposite sides of the chalkboard.

PRESENTATION

1. Point to the yarn at the top of pupil page 46 and then to the yarn on the chalkboard. Say *yarn* several times. Emphasize the sound of the *Y*. Do the same with *baby*.

2. Point to illustration #1 on pupil page 46. Say *Yard* with an emphasis on the *Y* sound. Ask the students whether the *Y* in *Yard* sounds like the *Y* in *yarn*. Does it sound like the *Y* in *baby*? Model circling the correct response under the illustration. Ask the students to do the same in their texts. Repeat with the remaining illustrations.

3. Have the students create a Language Experience Story (LES) by following these steps:

a. Write *baby* on the chalkboard. Model the word. Have students repeat. Ask individual students, *Do you have a baby? How old is your baby? What is her/his name?* As students respond to your questioning, write on the chalkboard, word for word, what each student dictates.

b. Have everyone listen carefully as you read, several times, what the student has dictated. As you read, point to (track) each word.

c. Now have all the students read the story on the board with you. Repeat this several times. Continue to point to (track) each word.

d. Next, begin hesitating before certain words, waiting for the students to orally fill in the words that are being omitted.

e. Now erase certain words in the story and, as you read, ask the students to orally supply the missing words. Fill in the blank spaces, as appropriate.

f. Put the sentences of the student composition on sentence strips, one sentence per strip. Scramble the sentences. The students must put the sentences in correct order.

g. Cut the strips into pieces, isolating individual words. Form several small groups of students. Distribute two or three sentence strips that have been cut into pieces to each group. Ask the groups to form new or original sentences from the cut-out words. Have the students write the dialogues in their spiral notebooks on page 46.

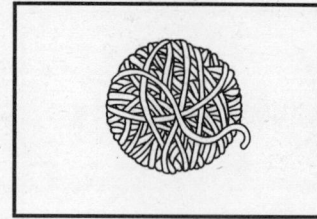

yarn

baby

1.	*yard*	2.	*strawberry*	3.	*yawn*
yarn (circled) baby		yarn baby (circled)		yarn (circled) baby	

4.	*Kentucky*	5.	*penny*	6.	*yucca*
yarn baby (circled)		yarn baby (circled)		yarn (circled) baby	

7.	*yield*	8.	*New Jersey*	9.	*yolk*
yarn (circled) baby		yarn baby (circled)		yarn (circled) baby	

46

cup

cereal

---

1. **celery**

cup (cereal)

2. **cat**

(cup) cereal

3. **car**

(cup) cereal

4. **cake**

(cup) cereal

5. **can**

(cup) cereal

6. **dice**

cup (cereal)

7. **pencil**

cup (cereal)

8. **comb**

(cup) cereal

9. **race**

cup (cereal)

47

OBJECTIVE

Students will differentiate the hard and soft sounds of *C*.

PREPARATION

Make photocopied enlargements of the illustrations at the top of pupil page 47. Attach the illustrations to opposite sides of the chalkboard.

PRESENTATION

1. Point to the cup at the top of pupil page 47 and then to the cup on the chalkboard. Say *cup* several times. Emphasize the sound of the *C*. Do the same with *cereal*.

2. Point to illustration #1 on pupil page 47. Say *celery* with an emphasis on the *C* sound. Ask the students whether the *C* in *celery* sounds like the *C* in *cereal*. Does it sound like the *C* in *cup*? Model circling the correct response under the illustration. Ask the students to do the same in their texts. Repeat with the remaining illustrations.

3. Have the students create a Language Experience Story (LES) by following these steps:

   a. Write *cereal* on the chalkboard. Model the word. Have students repeat. Ask individual students, *Do you eat cereal? What kind of cereal do you like?* As students respond to your questioning, write on the chalkboard, word for word, what each student dictates.

   b. Have everyone listen carefully as you read, several times, what the student has dictated. As you read, point to (track) each word.

   c. Now have all the students read the story on the board with you. Repeat this several times. Continue to point to (track) each word.

   d. Next, begin hesitating before certain words, waiting for the students to orally fill in the words that are being omitted.

   e. Now erase certain words in the story and, as you read, ask the students to orally supply the missing words. Fill in the blank spaces, as appropriate.

   f. Put the sentences of the student composition on sentence strips, one sentence per strip. Scramble the sentences. The students must put the sentences in correct order.

   g. Cut the strips into pieces, isolating individual words. Form several small groups of students. Distribute two or three sentence strips that have been cut into pieces to each group. Ask the groups to form new or original sentences from the cut-out words. Have the students write the dialogues in their spiral notebooks on page 47.

OBJECTIVE

Students will differentiate the hard and soft sounds of *G*.

PREPARATION

Make photocopied enlargements of the illustrations at the top of pupil page 48. Attach the illustrations to opposite sides of the chalkboard.

PRESENTATION

1. Point to the guitar at the top of pupil page 48 and then to the guitar on the chalkboard. Say *guitar* several times. Emphasize the sound of the *G*. Do the same with *giraffe*.

2. Point to illustration #1 on pupil page 48. Say *glass* with an emphasis on the *G* sound. Ask the students whether the *G* in glass sounds like the *G* in *guitar*. Does it sound like the *G* in *giraffe*? Model circling the correct response under the illustration. Ask the students to do the same in their texts. Repeat with the remaining illustrations.

3. Have the students create a Language Experience Story (LES) by following these steps:

a. Write *guitar* on the chalkboard. Model the word. Have students repeat. Ask individual students, *Do you play the guitar? What kind of music do you play? Tell me about it.* As students respond to your questioning, write on the chalkboard, word for word, what each student dictates.

b. Have everyone listen carefully as you read, several times, what the student has dictated. As you read, point to (track) each word.

c. Now have all the students read the story on the board with you. Repeat this several times. Continue to point to (track) each word.

d. Next, begin hesitating before certain words, waiting for the students to orally fill in the words that are being omitted.

e. Now erase certain words in the story and, as you read, ask the students to orally supply the missing words. Fill in the blank spaces, as appropriate.

f. Put the sentences of the student composition on sentence strips, one sentence per strip. Scramble the sentences. The students must put the sentences in correct order.

g. Cut the strips into pieces, isolating individual words. Form several small groups of students. Distribute two or three sentence strips that have been cut into pieces to each group. Ask the groups to form new or original sentences from the cut-out words. Have the students write the dialogues in their spiral notebooks on page 48.

guitar

giraffe

1. **glass**

(guitar)   giraffe

2. **page**

guitar   (giraffe)

3. **grapes**

(guitar)   giraffe

4. **hedge**

guitar   (giraffe)

5. **general**

guitar   (giraffe)

6. **gum**

(guitar)   giraffe

7. **giant**

guitar   (giraffe)

8. **gym**

guitar   (giraffe)

9. **gas**

(guitar)   giraffe

Picture worksheet (pupil page 49):

car	circle	cot
(cup) cereal	cup (cereal)	(cup) cereal

giant	gum	goat
guitar (giraffe)	(guitar) giraffe	(guitar) giraffe

bed	bee	key
(egg) eat	egg (eat)	egg (eat)

clock	robe	pot
(octopus) ocean	octopus (ocean)	(octopus) ocean

49

OBJECTIVE

Students will review letters with more than one sound.

PREPARATION

Cut paper into strips for writing sentences.

PRESENTATION

1. Ask students if they know the words for the pictures on the top half of pupil page 49. Supply words they don't know. Then ask the students to circle the written word that has the same beginning sound as the one representing the picture.

2. Do the same thing for vowel sounds at the bottom half of pupil page 49.

3. Have the students create a Language Experience Story (LES) by following these steps:

a. Write *circle* on the chalkboard. Model the word. Have students repeat. Ask individual students, *Name something with the shape of a circle. Describe it.* As students respond to your questioning, write on the chalkboard, word for word, what each student dictates.

b. Have everyone listen carefully as you read, several times, what the student has dictated. As you read, point to (track) each word.

c. Now have all the students read the story on the board with you. Repeat this several times. Continue to point to (track) each word.

d. Next, begin hesitating before certain words, waiting for the students to orally fill in the words that are being omitted.

e. Now erase certain words in the story and, as you read, ask the students to orally supply the missing words. Fill in the blank spaces, as appropriate.

f. Put the sentences of the student composition on sentence strips, one sentence per strip. Scramble the sentences. The students must put the sentences in correct order.

g. Cut the strips into pieces, isolating individual words. Form several small groups of students. Distribute two or three sentence strips that have been cut into pieces to each group. Ask the groups to form new or original sentences from the cut-out words. Have the students write the dialogues in their spiral notebooks on page 49.

OBJECTIVE

Students will recognize beginning, end, and middle as these concepts apply to position in line.

PREPARATION

Prepare a set of flash cards containing the students' first names.

PRESENTATION

Note: Throughout the exercises of *Entry to English Literacy Book 2*, students should be made aware that every word begins with a sound, that most words have an ending sound, and that many words have sounds in between. Students must learn to be discriminating in examining each part of a word. The eye can quickly see the beginning and end of the word, but it is more difficult to decode the middle. If a student can decode the beginning and end of a word, they have a much better chance of decoding the entire word correctly.

In the following lessons, students will look at letter sounds positioned in words in this order: Beginning, End, Middle.

1. Ask three students to form a line at your desk. Ask, *Who is at the beginning?* Have the correct student hold up his or her hand. Repeat the question using *end* and *middle*. Now say to the student at the end of the line, *Go to the beginning.* Wait for a physical response. Then say to the student at the end, *Go to the middle.* Then ask the third student, *Go to the end.* Repeat with several groups of students.

2. Use your name and students' names on the chalkboard to demonstrate the position of the middle name. Emphasize that it is positioned between two other names, the first and the last, very much like the middle person standing in line on pupil page 50. Have students write their full names in their notebooks, underlining their middle name if they have one.

3. Point to the picture at the top of pupil page 50. Indicate the person below the arrow and ask the students, *Beginning, middle, or end?* Demonstrate circling the word below the picture. Ask the students to do the same in their texts. Continue with the *middle* and *end* pictures.

4. Have the students create a Language Experience Story (LES) by asking the following questions: *Do you stand in line? Where do you stand in line?* Have the students write the dialogues in their spiral notebooks on page 50.

Beginning

End

Middle

50

CAT

C is at the <u>beginning</u> of the word.

T is at the <u>end</u> of the word.

A is in the <u>middle</u> of the word.

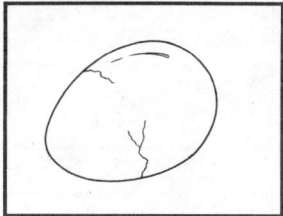

EGG

E is at the _____*beginning*_____ of the word.

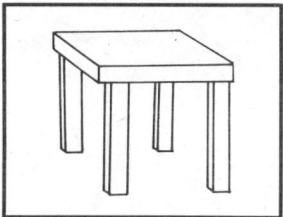

TABLE

E is at the _____*end*_____ of the word.

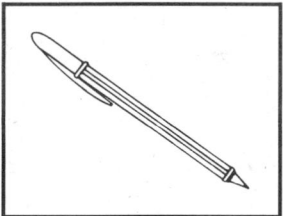

PEN

E is in the _____*middle*_____ of the word.

51

OBJECTIVE

Students will recognize beginning, middle, and end as these concepts apply to the position of letters in words.

PREPARATION

Prepare a set of flash cards with the following words: *cat, egg, table, pen.*

PRESENTATION

1. Attach the flash cards to the chalkboard vertically, as on pupil page 51. Point to the cat at the top of pupil page 51, then to the *cat* flash card on the chalkboard. Say, *The C is at the beginning of the word.* Have the students repeat. Ask them to track the letters as they read the words in their texts. Repeat with *A* and *T.*

2. Point to the egg on pupil page 51, then to the *egg* flash card on the chalkboard. Say, *The E is at the beginning of the word.* Model writing the word *beginning* in the correct space. Ask the students to do the same in their texts.

3. Point to the table, and to the table flash card. Say, *The E is at the end of the word.* Model writing the word *end* in the correct space. Ask the students to do the same in their texts.

4. Point to the pen, then to the pen flash card on the chalkboard. Say, *The E is in the middle of the word.* Model writing the word *middle* in the correct space. Ask the students to do the same in their texts.

5. Ask students to set up a row of chairs to simulate a bus. Ask students, one at a time, to take a seat at the beginning, end, or middle of the bus. Ask, *Is the driver at the beginning, end, or middle of the bus?*

6. Write *beginning, end, middle* on the chalkboard. Have the students create a group Language Experience Story (LES) about the bus ride. Ask, *Where was the bus at the beginning of the trip?* Write their answers under the *beginning* title on the chalkboard. Now ask, *Where is the train going to be at the end of the trip?* Write students' answers under the *end* section of the chalkboard. Finally, ask, *Where is the bus now?* Write students' answers under the *middle* title. Call out titles and ask students to read different sections. Then ask students to read the story in proper sequence: beginning, middle, end. Ask students to copy the story in this order in their spiral notebooks on page 51.

OBJECTIVE

Students will recognize beginning, middle, and end as these concepts apply to the position of letters in words.

PREPARATION

Be sure all students bring their texts.

PRESENTATION

1. Ask, *Is page one at the beginning, end, or middle of your book?* Ask the same questions for pages 4, 92, 44, 3, 89, 50, and 48. Ask students to turn to each page number as it is called. Circulate to check for comprehension.

2. At the top of pupil page 52, point to the key and ask students to read the words. Explain that *B, E,* and *M* stand for *beginning, end,* and *middle.*

3. Ask if students can read the words under the pictures. If not, supply the word. Ask, *Is the letter C at the beginning, end, or middle of the word* **coat**? Point to the circled *B* to indicate that the letter *C* is at the beginning. Do the next five examples together. Read the words under the remaining three pictures and ask students to circle the appropriate letters on their own, if possible.

4. On notebook page 52, ask students to write the name of the city they live in. Ask them to circle the letter at the beginning, at the end, and one letter in the middle.

B = Beginning   E = End   M = Middle

coat

(B) E M

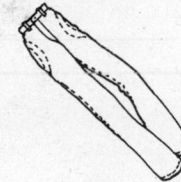

pants

(B) E M

shirt

B (E) M

dress

B E (M)

suit

(B) E M

cap

B E (M)

shoes

B (E) M

sweater

B (E) M

hat

B E (M)

52

Aa — apple

| a̲m | Ⓑ E M | Ri̲t̲a | B Ⓔ M |
| ba̲t | B E Ⓜ | tha̲t | B E Ⓜ |

Ee — elephant

| be̲d | B E Ⓜ | rice̲ | B Ⓔ M |
| e̲nd | Ⓑ E M | te̲a | B E Ⓜ |

Ii — ink

| mi̲lk | B E Ⓜ | I̲s | Ⓑ E M |
| ki̲ng | B E Ⓜ | i̲nch | Ⓑ E M |

Oo — fox

| go̲ | B Ⓔ M | ho̲t | B E Ⓜ |
| co̲ck | B E Ⓜ | o̲n | Ⓑ E M |

Uu — umbrella

| u̲s | Ⓑ E M | U̲tah | Ⓑ E M |
| tu̲b | B E Ⓜ | fu̲ | B Ⓔ M |

53

OBJECTIVE

Students will recognize beginning, middle, and end as these concepts apply to the position of letters in words.

PREPARATION

Write the following words on the chalkboard: *gum, bus, jet, soap, pencil.*

PRESENTATION

1. Write *B E M* on the chalkboard. Point to the letter *A* on the top row of pupil page 53. Now say, *apple.* Emphasize the sound of the *A.* Ask, *Is A at the beginning, end, or middle of* **apple**? Demonstrate circling the correct answer on the chalkboard. Now continue with the remaining words on pupil page 53. Ask the students to make the correct responses in their texts. circulate to check for comprehension.

2. Have the students copy the six words from the chalkboard, circle the ending letters, and read the words. Students have already studied the beginning sounds of these words.

3. On page 53 of their spiral notebooks, ask students to write the name of the state they live in and to circle the *B E M* letters (as they did on notebook page 52). Then ask students to write the name of the country they came from and again to circle the *B E M* letters.

OBJECTIVE

Students will review the concepts beginning, end, and middle.

PREPARATION

Prepare a set of flash cards containing the following words: *man, bed, fig, log, cup.*

PRESENTATION

1. Have students refer to the top exercise on pupil page 54. Ask students to circle the correct letter that indicates the position of the person in line.

2. For the second exercise, ask the students to circle the correct letter indicating the position of the pages in the book. Model the exercise using your textbook. Then have the students do the same in their texts.

3. On the chalkboard, reproduce the top row of the third exercise. Model circling the *B, E,* or *M* as indicated by the underlined letter. Ask the students to look at the word, find the underlined letter, decide if it is at the *beginning, end,* or *middle,* and circle *B, E,* or *M.*

4. On notebook page 54, ask students to copy the five words from the chalkboard. Have them circle the middle letters and read the words. Have students carefully look at and listen to the middle sounds of these words.

B E (M)

B E (M)

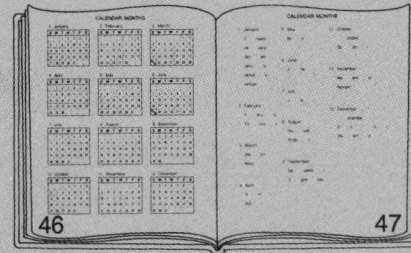

B E (M)

(B) E M

1. | answer | | airplan e | | bi ll |

(B) E M   B (E) M   B E (M)

2. | c a r | | b o y | | coffe e |

B E (M)   B E (M)   B (E) M

3. | ju g | | Lis a | | u se |

B E (M)   B (E) M   (B) E M

54

B

1.

(house)   mouse

B

2.

(cat)   bat

E

3.

bus   (rug)

E

4.

road   (top)

M

5.

cup   (cap)

M

6.

(pin)   pen

E

7.

pig   (pill)

M

8.

(beet)   boat

55

OBJECTIVE

Students will distinguish the beginning, middle, and end sounds in a given word.

PREPARATION

Draw a circle on the chalkboard and divide it three times so it looks like a pie cut into six pieces. Cut paper into strips for writing sentences.

PRESENTATION

1. Point to the uppercase *B* above the *house* and *mouse* at the top row of pupil page 55. Explain to the students that the *B* stands for *beginning*. Point to the *E* in the second row and explain that the *E* indicates *end*. Point to the *M* on the third row and explain that it indicates *middle*. Tell students that you will dictate a word. Ask students to circle the word under the picture that begins, ends, or has the same sound in the middle. Dictate: *1. horse 2. car 3. rag 4. pump 5. fat 6. sit 7. seal 8. feet*

2. Ask students to draw a circle in their spiral notebooks on page 55 like the one you drew on the chalkboard. Model writing six words in the circle on the chalkboard, one word per slice. Have the students copy six words from pupil page 55. Ask students to put one word in each slice of the "pie." Then, write the words *beginning, end*, and *middle* beneath your circle.

3. Read one of the words from pupil page 55. Write it to the side of your "pie" on the chalkboard. Then point to one of the following words on the chalkboard: *beginning, end, middle.* If students have a word that has the same sound in the position you are indicating, they cross out that section of their pie. For example, if you point to *beginning* and say *cat*, students should cross out any word beginning with the hard *C* sound. The first student to cross off all six sections wins. Ask the winner to read all six words in his or her circle. Have the class verify the winner's responses.

4. Have the students create a Language Experience Story (LES) by asking the following question: *Which road do you take to school? What do you see on that road?* Have the students write the dialogues in their spiral notebooks on page 55.

OBJECTIVE

Students will distinguish the beginning, middle, and end sounds in a given word.

PREPARATION

Create a set of alphabet flash cards for each group of four students. Cut paper into strips for writing sentences.

PRESENTATION

1. Point to the fish at the top of pupil page 56. Say *fish*. Emphasize the beginning sound. Ask the students to circle the *F* to the left of the picture if they hear *F* at the beginning of the word. Have them circle the *F* to the right of the picture if they hear the sound at the end of the word. Follow the same procedure for the remaining items. The first one is marked. Ask students to say the names of the pictures. Supply the words if needed. Do the first row together. Then ask the students to complete the remainder of the exercise on their own.

2. At the bottom of the page, ask students to write the letters in the blanks to complete the words under the pictures. They may refer to pupil pages 8-31 or to their notebooks.

3. Create groups of four students. Write *beginning, middle,* and *end* on the chalkboard. Give each group a set of alphabet flash cards. Now point to *beginning* on the chalkboard. Dictate a word from pupil page 56. Ask the groups to hold up the beginning letter of the dictated word. Have the groups verify each other's work. Continue the exercise with *end* and *middle*.

4. Have the students create a Language Experience Story (LES) by asking the following questions: *Have you ever been on a train? Did you enjoy it? Tell me about it.* Have the students write the dialogues in their spiral notebooks on page 56.

Pupil page 57

B	1. *hill* *pill*	2. *lock* *rock*
E	1. *bus* *buzz*	2. *map* *mat*
M	1. *map* *mop*	2. *pin* *pen*

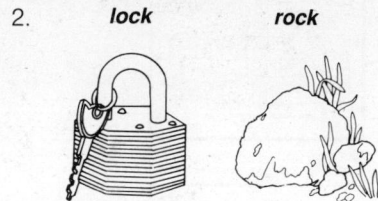

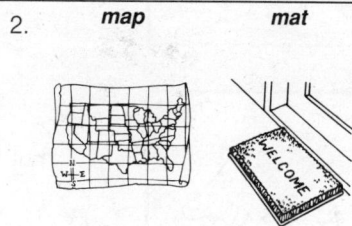

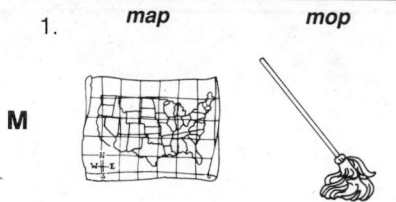

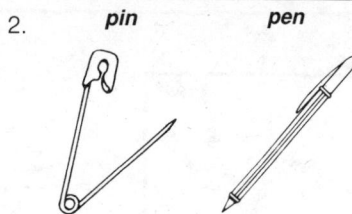

B	E	M
1. (a) e	1. f (p)	1. (a) e
2. b (d)	2. (t) b	2. (o) a
3. (r) l	3. (f) v	3. (u) i
4. (w) v	4. m (n)	4. (i) e

OBJECTIVE

Students will distinguish the beginning, middle, and end sounds in a given word.

PREPARATION

Create a set of flash cards indicating the following words: *hill, pill, lock, rock, bus, buzz, map, mat, map, mop, pin, pen.* These are minimal pairs—two words that are exactly the same, except for one sound. These minimal variations are difficult to discriminate and take repeated practice to distinguish.
Cut paper into strips for writing sentences.

PRESENTATION

1. Point to each picture on pupil page 57. As you point to each picture, hold up the flash card containing the appropriate word. Say the word clearly, and have the students repeat. Then say one word from each pair. Have the students circle the corresponding picture. Then, in the blank under each pair of pictures, have them write the letter that is different. In the first row, students will be listening for beginning sounds, indicated by the *B.* In the second row, they will listen for end sounds, *E.* In the third row, they will listen for middle sounds, *M.*

2. At the bottom of the page, dictate words and ask students to circle the letters they hear at the beginning, end, or middle of the words, as indicated by *B*, *E*, or *M* at the top of each column. Dictate:

B.	1. *answer*	2. *dark*	3. *road*	4. *war*
E.	1. *stop*	2. *bit*	3. *loaf*	4. *sun*
M.	1. *glad*	2. *pot*	3. *truck*	4. *kiss*

3. Show students one of the words from the sets of minimal pairs. Ask students to write the word for the other picture of the pair on notebook page 57. For example, show the *hill* flash card. The students should write the word *pill.* Ask the students to write any other words that sound like the dictated word in their spiral notebooks.

4. Have the students create a Language Experience Story (LES) by asking the following question: *What countries border (are next to) your native country? Show me on the map.* Have the students write the dialogues in their spiral notebooks on page 57.

OBJECTIVE

Students will distinguish the beginning and end sounds in a given word.

PREPARATION

Bring a set of alphabet flash cards. Write *beginning* and *end* on the chalkboard in uppercase letters. Cut paper into strips for writing sentences.

PRESENTATION

1. At the top of pupil page 58, ask students to look at the picture on the left. Say *bus*. Emphasize the beginning sound. Model circling the words on the right that have the same beginning sound. Pronounce each word clearly so that students can hear and locate the correct sounds. Students do not need to know the meanings of the words on the right, only to distinguish their sounds.

2. At the bottom of pupil page 58, ask students to look at the picture on the left. Say *leaf* with an emphasis on the end sound. Model circling the words on the right that have the same end sound. Pronounce each word so that students can hear and locate the correct sounds. Students do not need to know the meanings of the words on the right, only to distinguish their sounds.

3. Create groups of four students. Write *beginning*, and *end* on the chalkboard. Give each group a set of alphabet flash cards. Now point to *beginning* on the chalkboard. Dictate a word from pupil page 58. Ask the groups to hold up the beginning letter of the dictated word. Continue the exercise with *end*.

4. Have the students create a Language Experience Story (LES). Point to the stop sign at the bottom of pupil page 58 and ask the following questions: *What does this sign mean? What other signs do you know? What do they mean?* Have the students write the dialogues in their spiral notebooks on page 58.

58

B

1.  *bus*

   corn   (bat)   (ball)   table

2.  *ring*

   (road)   load   look   bill

3. 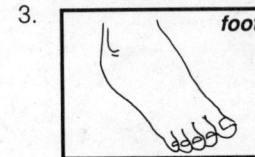 *foot*

   put   (fill)   book   pipe

E

1.  *leaf*

   (off)   go   sit   till

2.  *man*

   more   back   (woman)   (born)

3.  *stop*

   PUSH   BUS   (PUP)   PULL

58

1. milk

	M		
in	(this)	moon	wake

2. coat

tent	pants	(road)	lamp

3. belt

bill	book	(neck)	key

4. fan

top	lid	(that)	film

B	**E**	**M**
1. (r) l t	1. (p) f z	1. a e (u)
2. (w) v	2. t (d)	2. (a) e
3. (j) y	3. (s) z	3. (i) e
4. i (e)	4. e (v)	4. (o) u
5. _p_	5. _l_	5. _e_

59

OBJECTIVE

Students will distinguish the beginning, middle, and end sounds in a given word.

PREPARATION

Bring a set of alphabet flash cards.

PRESENTATION

1. At the top of pupil page 59, ask students to look at the picture and say the word *milk*. Ask students what words they can read on the right. Supply the words as needed. Students do not need to know the meanings of the words on the right, only to distinguish their sounds. Ask students to circle the words on the right that have the same middle sound as *milk*. Follow the same procedure for the remaining items.

2. At the bottom of the page, dictate words and ask the students to circle the letters they hear at the beginning, end, or middle of the words as indicated by B, E, or M at the top of each column. The last item (#5) in each column has no answer choice. Students must produce the written form of the letter they hear. Dictate:

B.	1. read	2. wife	3. jam	4. eagle	5.pepper
E.	1. sheep	2. bad	3. grass	4. love	5. sell
M.	1. fun	2. plate	3. sit	4. boat	5. teach

3. Create groups of four students. Write *beginning, middle,* and *end* on the chalkboard. Give each group a set of alphabet flash cards. Now point to *beginning* on the chalkboard. Dictate a word from pupil page 59. Ask the groups to hold up the beginning letter of the dictated word. Continue the activity with *end* and *middle*.

OBJECTIVE

Students will distinguish and write the beginning, middle, and end sounds in a given word.

PREPARATION

Bring a set of alphabet flash cards.

PRESENTATION

1. On pupil page 60, ask students to write the *beginning, middle,* and *end* sounds they hear as you dictate the following words:

B. 1. bill 2. kill 3. sill 4. dill 5. fill
   6. gill 7. hill 8. mill 9. pill 10. will
   11. jam 12. yam 13. dam 14. ham 15. ram
   16. pin 17. sin 18. bin 19. gin 20. fin

E. 1. cop 2. cob 3. cod 4. cot 5. cog
   6. can 7. cat 8. cap 9. cab 10. cad
   11. cam 12. sit 13. sin 14. six 15. sip
   16. sis

M. 1. nut 2. not 3. net 4. pet 5. pot
   6. pit 7. pat 8. fun 9. fan 10. fin
   11. bin 12. bun 13. ban

2. Explain to the students that the dictated words belong to *families* with the same letters at the beginning or end. Write *ill* on the chalkboard. Distribute the *p, d, f, g, h, m, p,* and *w* flash cards to various students. Dictate words from the exercise list and ask the student holding the initial consonant to hold up his or her flash card. Follow the same procedure with the *middle* and *end* cards. Have the students verify each other's work.

B

1. _b_ ill
2. _k_ ill
3. _s_ ill
4. _d_ ill
5. _f_ ill
6. _g_ ill
7. _h_ ill
8. _m_ ill
9. _p_ ill
10. _w_ ill

11. _j_ am
12. _y_ am
13. _d_ am
14. _h_ am
15. _r_ am

16. _p_ in
17. _s_ in
18. _b_ in
19. _g_ in
20. ___ in

E

1. co _p_
2. co _b_
3. co _d_
4. co _t_
5. co _g_

6. ca _n_
7. ca _t_
8. ca _p_
9. ca _b_
10. ca _d_
11. ca _m_

12. si _t_
13. si _n_
14. si _x_
15. si _p_
16. si _s_

M

1. n _u_ t
2. n _o_ t
3. n _e_ t

4. p _e_ t
5. p _o_ t
6. p _i_ t
7. p _a_ t

8. f _u_ n
9. f _a_ n
10. f ___ n

11. b _i_ n
12. b _u_ n
13. b _a_ n

60

B

1. cot	(dog)	call	car
2. pin	put	(sat)	pet
3. zip	zoo	zero	(sit)
4. wife	wine	(vine)	want
5. tame	time	tip	(lame)
6. line	(band)	limb	lady

E

1. cut	fat	(wig)	wet
2. if	off	leaf	(pup)
3. desk	(list)	risk	kick
4. bad	(bet)	sod	red
5. wag	dig	plug	(wax)
6. bend	had	(lab)	mad

M

1. van	fan	bad	(bud)
2. hit	big	(son)	rib
3. hop	(run)	pop	mom
4. bug	hug	cut	(cat)
5. beg	leg	(log)	bet
6. cane	came	rain	(vine)

61

OBJECTIVE

Students will distinguish the beginning, middle, and end sounds in a given word. Bring a set of alphabet flash cards for each group of four students.

PREPARATION

On the chalkboard, reproduce the exercises on pupil page 61.

PRESENTATION

1. Point to and read each word at the top of pupil page 61. Demonstrate circling the word that has a *different* beginning sound from word on the left. Emphasize *different*. Point out that the *B, E,* and *M* headings indicate the letter position stressed in each section. Demonstrate the first number in each exercise. Then do #2 - #4 as a class exercise. Ask students to do #5 - #6 on their own. Circulate to check for comprehension.

2. Ask the students to close their texts. Do the exercise on the page again orally and aurally. Point to and read the words on the chalkboard. The students should indicate the correct answer by raising their hands when you read the appropriate word. As a variation, ask them to indicate correct answers by standing up. This demands much more certainty from the student.

3. Create groups of four students. Write *beginning, middle,* and *end* on the chalkboard. Give each group a set of alphabet flash cards. Now point to *beginning* on the chalkboard. Dictate a word from pupil page 61. Ask the groups to hold up the beginning letter of the dictated word. Continue the exercise with *end* and *middle*.

OBJECTIVE

Students will distinguish and write the beginning, middle, and end sounds in a given word.

PREPARATION

Bring the alphabet flash cards.

PRESENTATION

1. On pupil page 62, dictate words and ask students to choose the correct letter at the right. Then ask them to write the letters in the appropriate blanks at the beginning, end, or middle of the words. Dictate:

| B. | 1. food | 2. war | 3. yam | 4. juice | 5. wife |
| | 6. had | 7. band | 8. jam | 9. toy | 10. load |

| E. | 1. Mom | 2. funny | 3. lamp | 4. bus | 5. rat |
| | 6. rob | 7. bag | 8. cow | 9. joy | 10. bad |

| M. | 1. sock | 2. pill | 3. miss | 4. fuzz | 5. tan |
| | 6. can | 7. new | 8. dime | 9. stop | 10. cut |

2. In the final exercise, ask students to write the missing letter in the word as you dictate it. Then ask them to supply *B, E,* or *M* in the blank following the word to show where that letter is positioned. Dictate:

| 1. tub | 2. zip | 3. heart | 4. vine | 5. lazy |
| 6. mice | 7. dine | 8. crazy | 9. hand | 10. bean |

3. Create groups of four students. Write *beginning, middle,* and *end* on the chalkboard. Give each group a set of alphabet flash cards. Now point to *beginning* on the chalkboard. Dictate a word at random from pupil page 62. Ask the groups to hold up the beginning letter of the dictated word. Continue the exercise with *end* and *middle*.

B

1. _f_ood	f	p	d
2. _w_ar	r	w	v
3. _y_am	j	y	h
4. _j_uice	j	z	
5. _w_ife	w	v	
6. _h_ad	h	j	
7. _b_and	b	c	
8. _j_am	w	j	
9. _t_oy	t	d	
10. _l_oad		l	

E

1. Mo_m_	m	n	g
2. funn_y_	v	y	g
3. lam_p_	f	p	t
4. bu_s_	s	z	
5. ra_t_	t	d	
6. ro_b_	b	g	
7. ba_g_	g	j	
8. co_w_	w	v	
9. jo_y_	z	y	
10. ba_d_		d	

M

1. s_o_ck	o	e	y
2. p_i_ll	i	e	a
3. m_i_ss	i	e	o
4. f_u_zz	i	u	
5. t_a_n	i	a	
6. c_a_n	e	a	
7. n_e_w	u	e	
8. d_i_me	i	y	
9. st_o_p	o	a	
10. c_u_t		u	

B E M

1. t_u_b	M
2. _z_ip	B
3. hear_t_	E
4. _v_ine	B
5. laz_y_	E
6. m_i_ce	M
7. d_i_ne	M
8. craz_y_	E
9. h_a_nd	M
10. bea_n_	E

Left page (pupil page 63)

1. zero

B   sand   (zoo)   bus   jar

2. mop

E   red   pull   (zip)   if

3. sun

M   (bus)   sin   us   call

B	E	M
1. a (e)	1. (p) f	1. (o) u
2. (r) l	2. t (d)	2. e (i)
3. _f_ ire	3. ga _s_	3. fe _e_ t
4. _y_ ear	4. fro _g_	4. h _i_ ll
5. _j_ ar	5. lea _f_	5. v _o_ te
6. _n_ ame	6. stree _t_	6. ph _o_ ne
7. _a_ ddress	7. cit _y_	7. y _e_ s

Right page

OBJECTIVE
Students will review the beginning, middle, and end sounds in given words.

PREPARATION
Bring the alphabet flash cards.

PRESENTATION

1. At the top of pupil page 63, ask students to look at the picture and say the word for the picture. Say words on the right and ask students to circle the one with the same *beginning, end,* or *middle* letter. The letters *B, E,* and *M* indicate the letter position being stressed in each row. Students do not need to know the meanings of words on the right, only to distinguish sounds.

2. At the bottom part of the page, ask students to listen for the *B, E,* or *M* sound as it is dictated. In #1 and #2 of each column, ask the students to circle the *B, E,* or *M* letter they hear in each word. For #3 - #7, ask students to write the appropriate letter in each blank. Dictate:

> B. *1. empty 2. rich 3. fire 4. year 5. jar 6. name 7. address*
>
> E. *1. shop 2. toad 3. gas 4. frog 5. leaf 6. street 7. city*
>
> M. *1. job 2. fine 3. feet 4. hill 5. vote 6. phone 7. yes*

3. Create groups of four students. Write *beginning, middle,* and *end* on the chalkboard. Give each group a set of alphabet flash cards. Now point to *beginning* on the chalkboard. Dictate a word from pupil page 63. Ask the groups to hold up the beginning letter of the dictated word. Continue the exercise with *end* and *middle.*

OBJECTIVE

Students will review distinguishing and writing the beginning, middle, and end sounds in given words.

PREPARATION

On the chalkboard, reproduce the second exercise on pupil page 64.

PRESENTATION

1. At the top of pupil page 64, ask the students to write in the appropriate blanks the beginning, end, and middle sounds that they hear. Dictate the following words:

B. *1. pet   2. wet   3. get   4. let   5. met   6. vet*

E. *1. bit   2. big   3. bib   4. bid   5. bin*

M. *1. him   2. ham   3. hum*

2. Point to and read each word in the second exercise on pupil page 64. On the chalkboard, demonstrate circling the word that has a *different* sound from the other words in the row. Emphasize *different*. Point out that the B, E, and M headings indicate the letter position stressed in each section. Model completing the first row, then have the students complete the remainder of the exercise in their texts. Circulate to check for comprehension.

3. Ask the students to close their texts. Do the exercise on the page again orally and aurally. Point to and read the words in the text. The students should indicate the correct answer by raising their hands when you read the appropriate word. As a variation, ask them to indicate correct answers by standing up.

	B	E	M
1.	__p__ et	bi __t__	h __i__ m
2.	__w__ et	bi __g__	h __a__ m
3.	__g__ et	bi __b__	h __u__ m
4.	__l__ et	bi __d__	
5.	__m__ et	bi __n__	
6.	__v__ et		

B

1.	fox	feel	(pet)	food
2.	(jam)	yet	you	yours
3.	letter	loan	leave	(bill)
4.	(day)	boat	bay	boy

E

1.	hop	zip	zap	(happy)
2.	mud	sad	(sun)	kid
3.	pet	let	get	(nod)
4.	cab	(bad)	lab	jab

M

1.	(bag)	red	get	pen
2.	Mom	hot	(put)	top
3.	(ten)	time	hide	gin
4.	gun	mule	cube	(cape)

DAYS OF THE WEEK

JUNE

1	2	3	4	5	6	7
Sunday	Monday	Tuesday	Wednesday	Thursday	Friday	Saturday
			1	2	3	4
5	6	7	8	9	10	11
12	13	14	15	16	17	18
19	20	21	22	23	24	25
26	27	28	29	30		

Sunday	Monday	Tuesday
Sunday	*Monday*	*Tuesday*

Wednesday	Thursday
Wednesday	*Thursday*

Friday	Saturday
Friday	*Saturday*

Monday ⌒ *Tuesday*
Thursday ⌒ *Friday*
Friday ⌒ Saturday
Saturday ⌒ *Sunday*

Monday ⌒ Tuesday
Tuesday ⌒ Wednesday
Friday ⌒ *Saturday*
Sunday ⌒ *Monday*

OBJECTIVE

Students will read and write the days of the week in correct sequential order.

PREPARATION

Bring a large calendar. Be sure the months are clearly written in uppercase letters. Create a set of flash cards indicating the days of the week.

PRESENTATION

1. Read *Days of the Week* at the top of pupil page 65. Have the students repeat. This is the first time in *Entry to English Literacy Book 2* that titles are used on a page. Ask the students to look at the tops of pages 65-66. Read *Days of the Week*. Explain that both of those pages have exercises about calendars.

2. Model *Calendar* and *Days of the Week*. Ask students to repeat. Demonstrate on the large calendar. Point out that the names of all days of the week end in the word *day* and that the pattern repeats every seven days.

3. On pupil page 65, ask the students to write the names of the days in the blanks provided. Next ask the students to write the name of the days that come before or after each printed day.

4. Distribute the flash cards, one each to seven students. To demonstrate the order of the days of the week, line up the students holding flash cards in proper sequential order. Repeat the exercise with different groups of students. Then mix up the flash cards and ask seven students to arrange themselves in proper sequential order.

5. Ask students to copy the days of the week in their spiral notebooks on page 65. Have them write the numbers 1-7 beneath the days.

OBJECTIVE

Students will correctly match the days of the week to their abbreviations.

PREPARATION

Cut paper into strips for writing sentences.

PRESENTATION

1. Model *Days of the Week* at the top of pupil page 66. Have students repeat in unison, then individually.

2. Point to the abbreviations used for days of the week on pupil page 66. Stress the standard abbreviations: *Sun., Mon., etc.* Ask students to draw lines matching the days of the week with the abbreviations. Then ask them to copy the abbreviations in the blanks. The first one is completed as an example.

3. At the bottom of the page, ask students to write abbreviations in the blanks that come before or after the printed abbreviation, as indicated by the arrows. The first blank is completed as an example. Watch for confusion between *Tues.* and *Thurs.*, and *Sat.* and *Sun.*

4. Have the students create a Language Experience Story (LES) by asking the following questions: *What days of the week do you attend class?* or *What do you usually do on Saturday?* Have the students write the dialogues in their spiral notebooks on page 66.

DAYS OF THE WEEK

JUNE

S	M	T	W	T	F	S
Sun.	Mon.	Tues.	Wed.	Thurs.	Fri.	Sat.
			1	2	3	4
5	6	7	8	9	10	11
12	13	14	15	16	17	18
19	20	21	22	23	24	25
26	27	28	29	30		

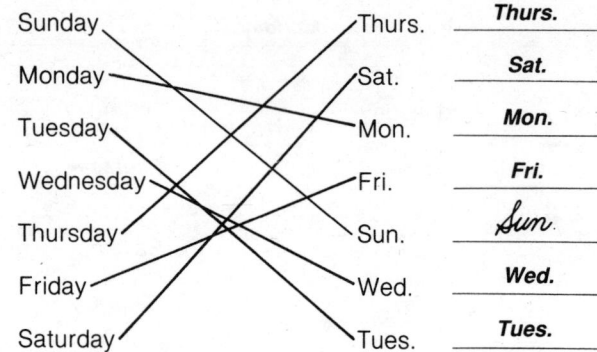

Sunday ——— Thurs.   ***Thurs.***
Monday ——— Sat.   ***Sat.***
Tuesday ——— Mon.   ***Mon.***
Wednesday ——— Fri.   ***Fri.***
Thursday ——— Sun.   *Sun.*
Friday ——— Wed.   ***Wed.***
Saturday ——— Tues.   ***Tues.***

Sun. ⌢ _____ *Mon.* _____   Wed. ⌢ _____ ***Thurs.*** _____

_____ ***Fri.*** _____ ⌢ Sat.   _____ ***Thurs.*** _____ ⌢ Fri.

Tues. ⌢ _____ ***Wed.*** _____   Thurs. ⌢ _____ ***Fri.*** _____

_____ ***Mon.*** _____ ⌢ Tues.   Fri. ⌢ _____ ***Sat.*** _____

MONTHS OF THE YEAR

1. January

   J__*a*__nuary

   Ja__*n*__uary

   Jan__*u*__ary

   Janu__*a*__ry

   Janua__*r*__y

   Januar__*y*__

   January

2. February

   F__*e*__bru__*a*__ry

   Fe__*b*__rua__*r*__y

   February

3. March

   Ma__*r*__ch

   Marc__*h*__

   March

4. April

   A__*p*__ril

   Apr__*i*__l

   April

5. May

   M__*a*__y

   May

6. June

   J__*u*__ne

   June

7. July

   J__*u*__ly

   July

8. August

   Au__*g*__ust

   Augu__*s*__t

   August

9. September

   Se__*p*__temb__*e*__r

   S__*e*__pte__*m*__ber

   September

10. October

    __*O*__ctober

    Oc__*t*__ob__*e*__r

    October

11. November

    No__*v*__em__*b*__er

    Novem__*b*__ __*e*__ __*r*__

    November

12. December

    __*D*__ecembe__*r*__

    D__*e*__c__*e*__ __*m*__b__*e*__r

    De__*c*__em__*b*__e__*r*__

    December

67

OBJECTIVE
Students will correctly write the months of the year.

PREPARATION
Bring the alphabet flash cards. Cut paper into strips for writing sentences.

PRESENTATION

1. Write *January* on the chalkboard. Point to (track) each letter. Have the students read the letters in unison. Do this several times. Then erase the letters at random. Ask the students to fill in the missing letters. Repeat the exercise using all twelve months.

2. Demonstrate filling in the missing letters for *January* on pupil page 67. Then have the students complete the exercises in their texts.

3. Write the twelve months on the chalkboard. Create groups of four students. Add *beginning, middle,* and *end* to the chalkboard. Give each group a set of alphabet flash cards. Now point to *beginning* on the chalkboard. Dictate a month. Ask the groups to hold up the beginning letter of the dictated month. Have the groups verify each other's work. Continue the exercise with *end* and *middle*.

4. Have the students create a Language Experience Story (LES) by asking the following questions: *Which months are the coldest? Which months are the warmest? Which month do you like? Why?* Have the students write the dialogues in their spiral notebooks on page 67.

OBJECTIVE

Students will match each month to its correct ordinal number.

PREPARATION

Bring a large calendar. Create a set of month flash cards, writing the name of each month on twelve separate cards.

PRESENTATION

1. Introduce ordinal numbers by pointing to and counting students at their desks. For example: *Beto is first. Marta is second. Angel is third.*

2. Model the phrase *Months of the Year* at the top of pupil page 68. Move from group to individual repetition.

3. Look at the names of the months on the calendar. Ask students to look at the calendars on pupil page 69 so that they can see all the months on one page. Point to each name as you say it. Ask students to repeat. Explain that the number of days in the months varies from 28 to 31. Explain that a month will not repeat again for one year. Ask, *How many days are in January? May? October? etc.*

4. Ask students to write the names of the months on notebook page 68. Write the months on the chalkboard. Erase random letters. Ask individuals to fill in the missing letters.

5. Distribute the cards to twelve students. To demonstrate the order of the months of the year, line up the students holding flash cards in proper sequential order. Ask individuals, *Which month is first? second? third? etc.* Repeat the exercise with different groups of students. Mix up the flash cards and ask twelve students to arrange themselves in proper sequential order.

6. Read the first sentence in exercise #1 on pupil page 68. Ask the students to give you the correct answer. Model circling the correct answer. Complete this exercise as a whole-class activity.

7. At the bottom of the page, ask students to circle the correct day. Have them use the calendars on pupil page 69 to determine their answers.

MONTHS OF THE YEAR

1. August is the ((8th), 3rd) month of the year.

2. February is the (1st, (2nd)) month of the year.

3. March is the (2nd, (3rd)) month of the year.

4. December is the (2nd, (12th)) month of the year.

5. July is the (11th, (7th)) month of the year.

6. October is the ((10th), 11th) month of the year.

7. June is the ((6th), 9th) month of the year.

8. January is the (11th, (1st)) month of the year.

9. April is the ((4th), 7th) month of the year.

10. May is the (3rd, (5th)) month of the year.

11. September is the (6th, (9th)) month of the year.

12. November is the (10th, (11th)) month of the year.

---

1. August 17 is on ((Saturday), Sunday).

2. May 21 is on (Wednesday, (Tuesday)).

3. January 13 is on ((Sunday), Monday).

4. October 17 is on (Tuesday, (Thursday)).

5. August 30 is on (Saturday, (Friday)).

6. February 6 is on (Tuesday, (Wednesday)).

7. December 25 is on ((Wednesday), Thursday).

8. June 1 is on (Sunday, (Saturday)).

MONTHS OF THE YEAR

1. Jan. _____ *Jan.*

S	M	T	W	T	F	S
		1	2	3	4	5
6	7	8	9	10	11	12
13	14	15	16	17	18	19
20	21	22	23	24	25	26
27	28	29	30	31		

2. Feb. _____ *Feb.*

S	M	T	W	T	F	S
					1	2
3	4	5	6	7	8	9
10	11	12	13	14	15	16
17	18	19	20	21	22	23
24	25	26	27	28		

3. Mar. _____ *Mar.*

S	M	T	W	T	F	S
					1	2
3	4	5	6	7	8	9
10	11	12	13	14	15	16
17	18	19	20	21	22	23
24/31	25	26	27	28	29	30

4. Apr. _____ *Apr.*

S	M	T	W	T	F	S
	1	2	3	4	5	6
7	8	9	10	11	12	13
14	15	16	17	18	19	20
21	22	23	24	25	26	27
28	29	30				

5. May _____ *May*

S	M	T	W	T	F	S
			1	2	3	4
5	6	7	8	9	10	11
12	13	14	15	16	17	18
19	20	21	22	23	24	25
26	27	28	29	30	31	

6. June _____ *June*

S	M	T	W	T	F	S
						1
2	3	4	5	6	7	8
9	10	11	12	13	14	15
16	17	18	19	20	21	22
23/30	24	25	26	27	28	29

7. July _____ *July*

S	M	T	W	T	F	S
	1	2	3	4	5	6
7	8	9	10	11	12	13
14	15	16	17	18	19	20
21	22	23	24	25	26	27
28	29	30	31			

8. Aug. _____ *Aug.*

S	M	T	W	T	F	S
				1	2	3
4	5	6	7	8	9	10
11	12	13	14	15	16	17
18	19	20	21	22	23	24
25	26	27	28	29	30	31

9. Sept. _____ *Sept.*

S	M	T	W	T	F	S
1	2	3	4	5	6	7
8	9	10	11	12	13	14
15	16	17	18	19	20	21
22	23	24	25	26	27	28
29	30					

10. Oct. _____ *Oct.*

S	M	T	W	T	F	S
		1	2	3	4	5
6	7	8	9	10	11	12
13	14	15	16	17	18	19
20	21	22	23	24	25	26
27	28	29	30	31		

11. Nov. _____ *Nov.*

S	M	T	W	T	F	S
					1	2
3	4	5	6	7	8	9
10	11	12	13	14	15	16
17	18	19	20	21	22	23
24	25	26	27	28	29	30

12. Dec. _____ *Dec.*

S	M	T	W	T	F	S
1	2	3	4	5	6	7
8	9	10	11	12	13	14
15	16	17	18	19	20	21
22	23	24	25	26	27	28
29	30	31				

69

OBJECTIVE

Students will read and write abbreviations for each month.

PREPARATION

Bring a large calendar. Create flash cards indicating the abbreviations for each month.

PRESENTATION

1. Read *Months of the Year* at the top of the page. Ask individual students to repeat. Move from individual to group response.

2. Point to and read each month on pupil page 69. Have the students repeat. Model copying the abbreviations of the months onto the lines. Ask the students to do the same in their texts. Circulate to check for comprehension.

3. Distribute the cards to twelve students. To demonstrate the abbreviations for the months of the year, line up the students holding flash cards in proper sequential order. Ask individuals, *Who has the card for May? November? July? etc.* Repeat the exercise with different groups of students. Ask the students to arrange themselves in proper sequential order.

4. Dictate months at random and have the students write the correct abbreviation in their spiral notebooks on page 69. Have the students verify each other's work.

OBJECTIVES

Students will correctly match ordinal numbers to each month. Students will read and write abbreviations for each month.

PREPARATION

Make and photocopy a 9-square grid (like a tic-tac-toe grid).

PRESENTATION

1. At the top of pupil page 70, ask the students to match ordinal numbers with the names of the months. Then ask them to copy the name of the month in the blank. The first one is completed as an example.

2. At the bottom of the page, ask students to match the name of the month with its abbreviation. Then ask the students to copy the abbreviation in the blank.

3. Distribute the photocopied grids. Ask students to write the names of months at random in the spaces. Each student's grid will be different. Read the names of the months. If students have the month you dictate written on their grids, have them mark an *X* on it. The first one to complete a row wins. Ask individual students to be readers for new games.

4. Ask students to choose one month and to write a Language Experience Story (LES) about what they usually do during that month. Ask questions such as, *What do you do in July? Do you swim? Do you eat ice cream? Do you wear a coat? Do you go on vacation?* Have the students write the dialogues in their spiral notebooks on page 70.

MONTHS OF THE YEAR

1st	November	*November*
2nd	June	*June*
3rd	February	*February*
4th	October	*October*
5th	January	*January*
6th	May	*May*
7th	September	*September*
8th	December	*December*
9th	March	*March*
10th	August	*August*
11th	April	*April*
12th	July	*July*

January	Apr.	*Apr.*
February	Aug.	*Aug.*
March	Oct.	*Oct.*
April	Dec.	*Dec.*
August	Sept.	*Sept.*
September	Jan.	*Jan.*
October	Mar.	*Mar.*
November	Feb.	*Feb.*
December	Nov.	*Nov.*

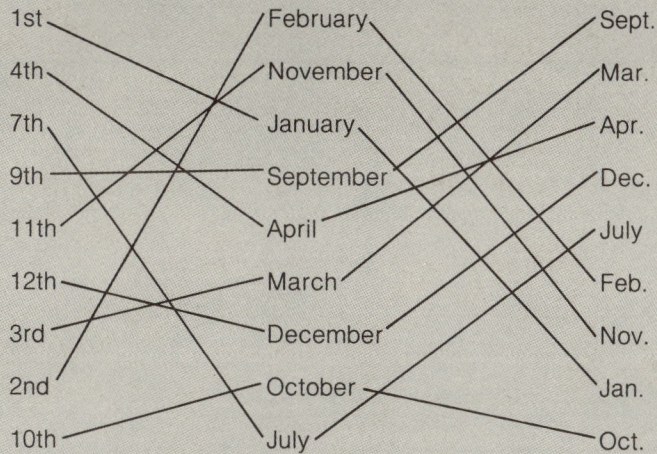

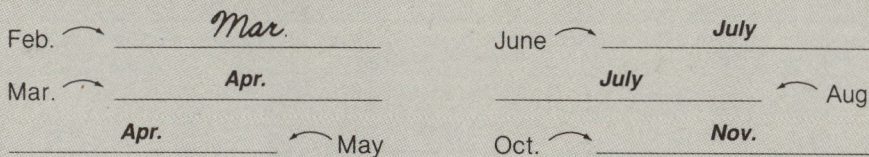

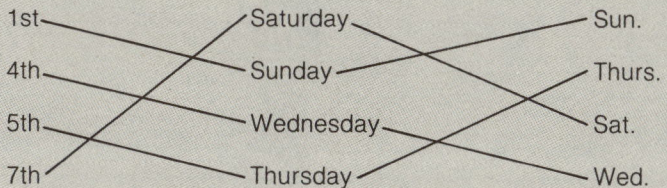

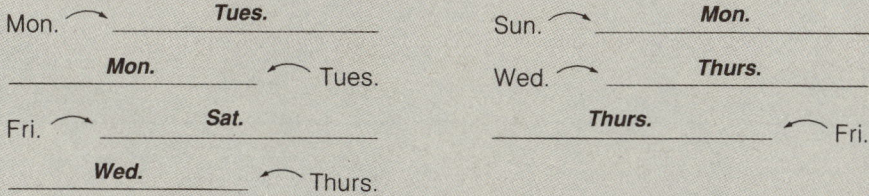

Worksheet (pupil page 71)

Match ordinal numbers to months, and months to abbreviations:

1st	February	Sept.
4th	November	Mar.
7th	January	Apr.
9th	September	Dec.
11th	April	July
12th	March	Feb.
3rd	December	Nov.
2nd	October	Jan.
10th	July	Oct.

Write abbreviations before or after, as indicated by arrows:

Feb. → _____ *Mar.*

Mar. → _____ *Apr.*

_____ *Apr.* ← May

June → _____ *July*

_____ *July* ← Aug.

Oct. → _____ *Nov.*

Match ordinal numbers to days, and days to abbreviations:

1st	Saturday	Sun.
4th	Sunday	Thurs.
5th	Wednesday	Sat.
7th	Thursday	Wed.

Write abbreviations before or after, as indicated by arrows:

Mon. → _____ *Tues.*

_____ *Mon.* ← Tues.

Fri. → _____ *Sat.*

_____ *Wed.* ← Thurs.

Sun. → _____ *Mon.*

Wed. → _____ *Thurs.*

_____ *Thurs.* ← Fri.

OBJECTIVE

Students will review correctly matching ordinal numbers to each month. Students will review reading and writing names and abbreviations of months and days.

PREPARATION

Cut paper into strips for writing sentences. On the chalkboard, reproduce the first exercise on pupil page 71.

PRESENTATION

1. For the first exercise, model matching ordinal numbers with names of months and then matching months with their abbreviations. Ask the students to complete the exercise in their texts. Circulate to check for comprehension.

2. For the next exercise, ask students to write the abbreviations of months that come before or after the printed abbreviations, as indicated by the arrows.

3. Next, ask students to match ordinal numbers with names of days and then to match the names with the abbreviations.

4. In the final exercise, ask students to write abbreviations of days in the blanks that come before or after the printed abbreviations, as indicated by the arrows.

5. Have the students create a group Language Experience Story (LES) by asking the following questions: *What do you do in March? April?* Record their answers on the chalkboard. For example: *Stephen plants a garden in March. He also goes to school.* Ask students to copy the LES in their spiral notebooks on page 71.

6. Photocopy the LES for each student. Cut the sentences apart. Give a set to each student and ask them to place the sentences in order. Ask, *Which sentence is first? second? etc.* Ask individuals to read the story when it is reassembled.

7. Use one sentence from the story. Cut phrases from sentences and give a set to each student. Try to give each student the sentence about him or herself. Ask students to reassemble the sentences. Ask individuals to read the sentences.

OBJECTIVE

Students will read and write dates.

PREPARATION

Bring a large calendar.

PRESENTATION

1. Read the heading *Calendar Dates* at the top of pupil page 72. Ask students to look at the headings on pages 72-73. Point out that both pages are about calendar dates.

2. On pupil page 72, point to the sentences in the illustrations. Ask students to follow in their texts while you read, *Please write today's date.*

3. Ask, *Are the words DAYS and DATES the same?* Explain that the days are Monday through Sunday, and that dates include the day, the month, and the year.

4. On pupil page 72, demonstrate where the date is located on the calendar to the left of the illustration. Point out that it is circled. Demonstrate that the way the date is written on the chalkboard in the illustration is the same as the date on the calendar. Ask students to fill in the current year. Ask students to write the two forms of dates in the blanks under the illustrations. Note: In many countries, the year is written first. In other countries, the day is written before the month. Watch for these transpositions.

5. Emphasize the two ways to write a date. On the chalkboard, model writing today's date in both ways. Ask students to write today's date several times (using both forms) in their spiral notebooks on page 72.

CALENDAR DATES

Answers will vary.

CALENDAR DATES

August 1991

Sunday	Monday	Tuesday	Wednesday	Thursday	Friday	Saturday
				1	②	3
4	5	6	⑦	8	9	10
11	12	13	14	⑮	16	17
⑱	19	20	21	22	23	24
25	26	㉗	28	29	30	㉛

August 2, 1991   8-2-91   **August 18, 1991**   *8-18-91*

August 7, 1991   *8-7-91*   **August 27, 1991**   *8-27-91*

August 15, 1991   *8-15-91*   **August 31, 1991**   *8-31-91*

December 1991

Sun.	Mon.	Tues.	Wed.	Thurs.	Fri.	Sat.
①	2	3	4	5	6	7
8	9	10	11	12	⑬	14
15	⑯	17	18	19	20	21
22	23	24	25	26	27	㉘
29	30	31				

December 1, 1991   12-1-91   **December 16, 1991**   *12-16-91*

December 13, 1991   *12-13-91*   **December 28, 1991**   *12-28-91*

73

OBJECTIVE

Students will correctly read and write dates.

PREPARATION

Bring the set of month flash cards that you created for pupil page 68. Create a set of date flash cards by writing the numbers 1-31 on separate index cards. Also make a set of year flash cards to be used in the Concentration game below.

PRESENTATION

1. Read the heading *Calendar Dates* at the top of pupil page 73. Ask students to look at the headings on pages 72-73. Point out that both pages are about calendar dates.

2. Direct the students' attention to the calendars on pupil page 73. Ask them to write in the blanks the two forms of the dates of circled days on the calendars. Reinforce orally:

Ask,   What day is it?   Answer,   "It's Friday."
"What's the date?"   "It's August 2nd, 1991."
"Is it the 2nd?"   "Yes, it is."
"Is it Monday?"   "No, it's Friday."
"Is it the 14th?"   "No, it's the second."

3. On spiral notebook page 73, ask students to write:

   1. Today's date.
   2. The date student came to the U.S.
   3. Student's birthdate.
   4. The date of student's marriage. (Optional)
   5. The date student moved to_____.

4. Play Concentration. Lay the date cards face down on the table. Ask students to turn over three cards on their first turn. For following turns, students discard one card and draw another until they get a complete date, such as January 1, 1992. Then they keep the completed set. When they get a complete date, they should draw three cards and start again. Students should never have more than three cards at a time, except for their completed sets. The person with the most completed sets wins.

73

OBJECTIVE
Students will review writing dates of birth.

PREPARATION
On the chalkboard, write your own birthdate and all students' birthdates. Have student records available, if possible. Cut paper into strips for writing sentences.

PRESENTATION

1. On pupil page 74, model writing your spouse's name and date of birth. Then fill in the blanks for your children's names and dates of birth. If you are single or have no children, use a married student's spouse and his or her children's names and birthdates. Use personal data files if student does not know birthdates. Write children's names in order, according to sequence of birth.

2. Ask students to fill in the blanks that apply to them. If they aren't married or do not have children, ask them to interview someone in the class who does. Have them fill in the blanks with that person's information.

3. For reinforcement, ask students: *How old are you? What is your age? What is your birthdate? When were you born?* Ask the same questions about the students' spouses, children, or friends. Have the students ask each other the questions.

4. Have the students create a Language Experience Story (LES) by asking the following questions: *Where were you born? Were you born in a hospital? Was a doctor there?* In this LES, make suggestions to help students write complete sentences, but try not to change the meaning students intended. Ask them if the changes are acceptable. Have the students write the dialogues in their spiral notebooks on page 74.

Spouse

Answers will vary.

_____   _____
Name   Date of Birth

Children

1st _____   _____
Name   Date of Birth

2nd _____   _____
Name   Date of Birth

3rd _____   _____
Name   Date of Birth

4th _____   _____
Name   Date of Birth

5th _____   _____
Name   Date of Birth

6th _____   _____
Name   Date of Birth

74

TIME

1. What time is it?	2. What time is it?	3. What time is it?
4:45	*6:30*	*12:00*
4. What time is it?	5. What time is it?	6. What time is it?
10:15	*9:00*	*5:45*

75

OBJECTIVE

Students will read clocks and tell the correct time in hours, quarter hours, and half hours.

PREPARATION

Use a real clock that will be visible to the entire class. Have the following materials available for each student to make a clock: paper plates, brass fasteners, and cardboard hands.

PRESENTATION

1. Read the heading *Time* at the top of pupil page 75. Ask students to look at the headings on pages 75-81. Point out that all of these pages are about time.

2. Create groups of four students. Give each group the materials for making a clock. Demonstrate by drawing the numbers on the paper plate and fastening the hands on with the brass fastener. Use the real clock as a model.

3. Write these words on the chalkboard: *clock, short hand, long hand, hour,* and *minutes.* Demonstrate on the real clock. Ask students to repeat the words after you. Elicit physical responses with commands such as: *Point to the clock. Turn the long hand. Turn the short hand.*

4. Set the real clock. Have the students set their clocks to the same time. Ask, *What time is it?* Have the students respond, *It is 3 o'clock.* Do not use smaller units than quarter hours. Change time settings and repeat. Teach different forms of answers: *3:15, 15 minutes after three, a quarter after three.* Do the same for half and three-quarter hours. Finally, set the clock to the current time. Have students do the same. Ask students to write the current time in their spiral notebooks on page 75. Be sure that they include a variety of forms presented in this lesson.

5. Demonstrate writing the correct time in the blank space below each illustration on pupil page 75. Ask the students to write the correct times in their texts.

OBJECTIVE

Students will read clocks and tell the correct time in hours, quarter hours, and half hours.

PREPARATION

Use a real clock and the clocks made by students in the previous lesson. Cut paper into strips for writing sentences.

PRESENTATION

1. Read the heading *Time* at the top of pupil page 76. Ask students to look at the headings on pages 75-81. Point out that these pages are about time.

2. Dictate the time on one clock in each box. Have students mark an *X* on the appropriate clock. Circulate and check for comprehension.

3. Set the real clock to 1:30. Have the students set their clocks to the same time. Ask, *What time is it?* Have the students respond, *It is one-thirty*. Teach different forms: *1:30, 30 minutes after one, half past one*. Finally, set the clock to the current time. Have students do the same. Ask students to write the current time in their spiral notebooks on page 76.

4. Have the students create a Language Experience Story (LES) by asking the following questions: *What time does class start? What time do you go to work?* In this LES, make suggestions to help students write complete sentences, but try not to change the meaning students intended. Ask them if the changes are acceptable. Have the students write the dialogues in their spiral notebooks on page 76.

TIME

1. What time is it?

2. What time is it?

3. What time is it?

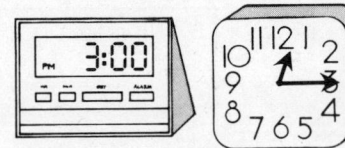

4. What time is it?

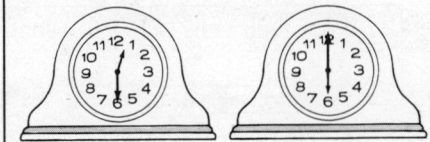

5. What time is it?

6. What time is it?

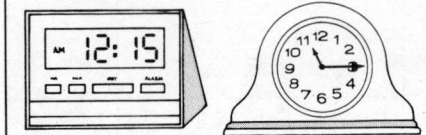

7. What time is it?

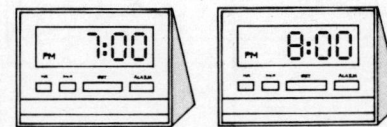

8. What time is it?

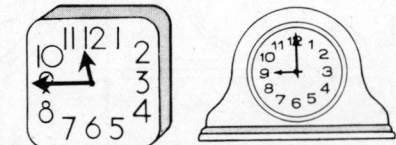

76

TIME

1. What time is it?	2. What time is it?	3. What time is it?
1:00	11:45	(2:15)
3 o'clock	(6 o'clock)	11:30
(5:45)	5:00	11:00

4. Is it 4:00?	5. Is it 5:15?	6. Is it 10:45?
Yes, it is.	Yes, it is.	(Yes, it is.)
(No, it isn't.)	(No, it isn't.)	No, it isn't.

7. What time is it?	8. What time is it?
6:00 *7:00*	*3:15* *6:15*

OBJECTIVE

Students will read clocks and tell the correct time in hours, quarter hours, and half hours.

PREPARATION

Use a real clock and the clocks made by students in the previous lesson. Cut paper into strips for writing sentences.

PRESENTATION

1. Read the heading *Time* at the top of pupil page 77. Ask students to look at the headings on pages 75-81. Point out that all these pages are about time.

2. Set the real clock to the current time. Ask yes/no questions, such as: *Is it 3 o'clock? Is it 7:30? Is it 11:15?* Elicit, *No, it isn't.* Then give the correct time and elicit, *Yes, it is.* Change time settings and repeat the procedure until students have mastered this skill.

3. Model circling the correct time beneath each illustration in #1 - #3 on pupil page 77. For items #4 - #6, ask students to circle the correct response. For items #7 - #8, ask students to write the time below the clocks.

4. Have the students create a Language Experience Story (LES) by asking the following questions: *What time do you finish work? What time do you eat dinner?* In this LES, make suggestions to help students write complete sentences, but try not to change the meaning students intended. Ask them if the changes are acceptable. Have the students write the dialogues in their spiral notebooks on page 77.

OBJECTIVE

Students will read and understand the concepts of a.m. and p.m.

PREPARATION

Use student clocks. Draw two clocks on the chalkboard. Photocopy a calendar for the present month with boxes for each day that are big enough for the students to write in.

PRESENTATION

1. Explain to the students that there are 24 hours in a day and that the hour hand goes around the clock face twice. This divides the day into two parts. Time during the first part of the day is shown by the letters A.M. Time during the second part of the day is shown by the letters P.M. Shade one of the clocks on the chalkboard to demonstrate P.M. and leave the other clock clear to demonstrate A.M.

2. Model the conversations in the pictures on pupil page 78. Ask the students to repeat. Ask the question and ask students to answer. Then ask students to do both parts of the conversation. Demonstrate copying the correct time below each illustration including A.M. and P.M. notations. Have the students do the same in their texts.

3. Distribute the calendars. Ask students, *What time did you come to class today?* Ask students to write their answers in their spiral notebooks on page 78. For example: *Class: 8:00 P.M.* Then ask students to copy their answers in the appropriate box (that is, today's box) on the photocopied calendars.

4. Ask, *What are you doing tomorrow?* Have students write answers in their notebooks and on their calendar copies. For example: *Doctor: 2:30 P.M.* After they gain confidence, ask students to notate appointments and planned activities for that week on their photocopies. Supply any vocabulary that students may need to complete this exercise.

5. When they have completed the calendar, photocopy each student's schedule so that he/she will have two copies. Tell them to glue one copy in their notebooks and to take the other copy home and place it where it is easily visible.

TIME

6:45 A.M.

6:45 A.M.

_____

9:00 A.M.

9:00 A.M.

_____

2:30 P.M.

2:30 P.M.

_____

TIME

6:30 P.M.

6:30 P.M.

10:30 P.M.

10:30 P.M.

12:00 noon

12:00 noon

12:00 midnight

12:00 midnight

79

OBJECTIVE

Students will read and understand the concepts of a.m., p.m., noon, and midnight.

PREPARATION

Use student clocks.

PRESENTATION

1. Write the following words on the chalkboard: *noon, midnight.* Have the students repeat the words after you several times. Explain to the students: *12:00 comes twice in one day. At midnight, the day begins. At noon, the day is halfway over. Then midnight returns. One day ends. A new day begins.*

2. Model the dialogues on pupil page 79 with an advanced student. Then have the students practice the dialogues in pairs. Demonstrate copying the correct time below each illustration, including the *A.M.* and *P.M.* notations. Have the students do the same in their texts.

3. Write the following actions on the chalkboard: *Eat lunch. Go to sleep. Go to class. Take a shower. Go shopping.* Ask students to choose one activity and to demonstrate the concept by drawing simple illustrations in their spiral notebooks on page 79. Now call out *noon* and *midnight* at random. Ask students to tell you when they would most likely be performing the activity they have illustrated.

4. Have the students create a Language Experience Story (LES) by asking the following questions: *What are you doing at noon? What are you doing at midnight?* In this LES, make suggestions to help students write complete sentences, but try not to change the meaning students intended. Ask them if the changes are acceptable. Have the students write the dialogues in their spiral notebooks on page 79.

OBJECTIVE

Students will correctly respond to questions about time.

PREPARATION

Use student clocks. Draw two clocks on the chalkboard. Photocopy a calendar for the present month with boxes for each day large enough for the students to write in.

PRESENTATION

1. Review with the students that there are 24 hours in a day and that the hour hand goes around the clock face twice. Shade one of the clocks on the chalkboard to show *P.M.* and leave the other clock clear to show *A.M.*

2. Model the questions above the illustrations on pupil page 80. Ask the students to repeat. Then ask individual students the questions and have them answer. Model correct responses. Ask students to circle correct responses in their texts.

3. Distribute the calendars. Ask students, *What time did you wake up this morning?* Ask students to write their answers in their spiral notebooks on page 80. For example: *Wake up: 7:00 A.M.* Then ask students to copy their answers in the appropriate box (that is, today's box) on the photocopied calendars.

4. Ask, *What time do you eat breakfast?* Have students write answers in their notebooks and on their calendar copies. For example: *Breakfast: 7:30 A.M.* After they gain confidence, ask students to notate appointments and planned activities for the next week on their photocopies. Supply any vocabulary that students may need to complete this exercise.

5. When they have completed the calendar, photocopy each student's schedule so that he/she will have two copies. Tell students to glue one copy in their notebooks and to take the other copy home and place it where it is easily visible.

TIME

1. Is it 5:15 P.M.?

(Yes, it is.)
No, it isn't.

2. Is it 7:45 A.M.?

Yes, it is.
(No, it isn't.)

3. Is it 12:15 P.M.?

(Yes, it is.)
No, it isn't.

4. Is it 8:30 P.M.?

(Yes, it is.)
No, it isn't.

5. Is it 11:30 A.M.?

(Yes, it is.)
No, it isn't.

6. Is it 5:30 A.M.?

(Yes, it is.)
No, it isn't.

TIME

1. 2:45 P.M.

12:00 noon

2. 7:30 A.M.

5:45 P.M.

10:30 P.M.

3. 12:00 midnight

9:15 A.M.

8:45 P.M.

4. 5 o'clock A.M.

6:15 P.M.

5. 11:45 P.M.

81

OBJECTIVE

Students will review reading clocks and telling the correct time in hours, quarter hours, and half hours.

PREPARATION

Draw a large tic-tac-toe grid on a sheet of paper. Photocopy a grid for each student.

PRESENTATION

1. Point to each illustration at the left of pupil page 81. Ask individual students to explain what is happening in the illustrations. Ask the students to suggest a time of day when the actions in the illustrations might be taking place.

2. Demonstrate matching the clocks in the center to the correct time on the right. Have the students do the same in their texts.

3. Write the following actions on the board: *Get up. Go to bed. Get dressed. Go to sleep. Go to class. Take a shower. Eat breakfast. Eat lunch. Eat dinner. Go shopping. Cook dinner. Wash dishes. Get on the bus. Get off the bus.* Distribute grids. Ask students to write *A.M.*, *P.M.*, *noon*, and *midnight* at random on the grids. Read actions and ask students to mark an *X* on the appropriate time of day that these actions take place. The first student to complete a row wins.

4. Have the students create a Language Experience Story (LES) by asking the following questions: *What time do you study English? What time do you usually go to sleep?* In this LES, make suggestions to help students write complete sentences, but try not to change the meaning students intended. Ask them if the changes are acceptable. Have the students write the dialogues in their spiral notebooks on page 81.

OBJECTIVE

Students will associate the letter symbol *ch* with the appropriate sound.

PREPARATION

Bring the alphabet flash cards. Prepare a set of flash cards containing the following words: *chair, match, cheese, children, watch, sandwich.* Add three sheets of newsprint to the wall charts. Write *ch, sh,* and *th* on each sheet.

PRESENTATION

1. Ask students to name the letters in the boxes at the top of pupil page 82. Have them write the letters several times in their spiral notebooks on page 82.

2. Hold up the *chair* flash card and say *chair.* Emphasize the sound of the *ch.* Ask the students to repeat the sound several times. Point from the flash card to the picture on pupil page 82 while repeating *chair.* Ask the students to write the word in their spiral notebooks. Repeat this procedure with the other words and pictures on pupil page 82.

3. Ask students to raise their hands if their first or last names begin with the same sound heard in the words they just learned. Write those names on the *ch* newsprint sheet. Ask if students know any other names that begin with the *ch* sound. Ask them to write those names on the chalkboard. Help them with the spelling. Underline the beginning letter. If their names don't begin with *ch,* let them write their names anyway and discover that they do not begin with *ch.* Students can erase the names that don't begin with *ch* from the chalkboard. Names that begin with *ch* can be added to the newsprint sheet. Encourage students to keep adding names or words that begin or end with *ch* to the newsprint sheets.

4. Ask students to choose one *ch* word from the newsprint sheet to write in their spiral notebooks on page 82. Encourage illustration. This word will be their key word to remember the sound that *ch* makes.

5. Direct the students' attention to the exercise at the bottom of pupil page 82. Explain that you will dictate a list of words. If the word contains the *ch* sound, they should circle the *ch* beside the appropriate number. If the word does not contain the *ch* sound, they should mark an *X* over the letters. Dictate: *1. much 2. chase 3. spell 4. benches 5. cheek 6. chin 7. horse 8. reaches 9. can.*

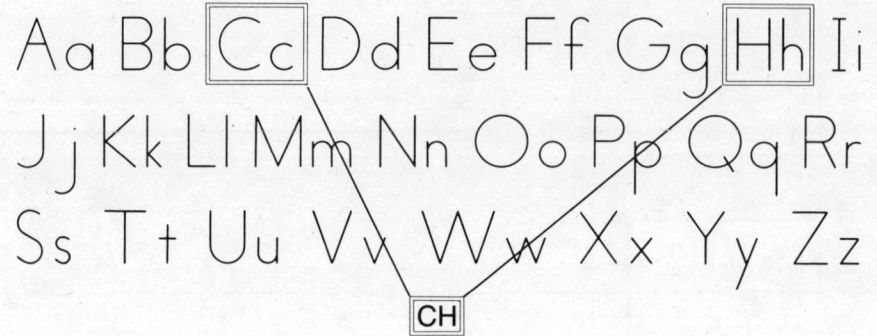

CH

chair

match

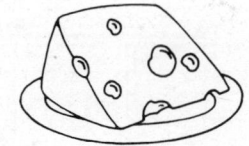

cheese

children

watch

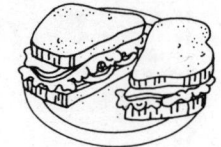

sandwich

1. (ch)   2. (ch)   3. ✗✗

4. (ch)   5. (ch)   6. (ch)

7. ✗✗   8. (ch)   9. ✗✗

SH

A a B b C c D d E e F f G g [H h] I i

J j K k L l M m N n O o P p Q q R r

[S s] T t U u V v W w X x Y y Z z

[SH]

sheep

shell

fish

shovel

shoe

brush

1. ✗   2. (sh)   3. (sh)

4. ✗   5. (sh)   6. ✗

7. (sh)   8. (sh)   9. (sh)

83

OBJECTIVE

Students will associate the letter symbol *sh* with the appropriate sound.

PREPARATION

Bring the alphabet flash cards. Prepare a set of flash cards containing the following words: *sheep, shell, fish, shovel, shoe, brush.*

PRESENTATION

1. Ask students to name the letters in the boxes at the top of pupil page 83. Have them write the letters several times in their spiral notebooks on page 83.

2. Hold up the *sheep* flash card and say *sheep*. Emphasize the sound of the *sh*. Ask the students to repeat the sound several times. Point from the flash card to the picture on pupil page 83 while repeating *sheep*. Ask the students to write the word in their spiral notebooks. Repeat this procedure with the other words and pictures on pupil page 83.

3. Ask students to raise their hands if their first or last names begin with the same sound heard in the words they just learned. Write those names on the *sh* newsprint sheet. Ask if students know any other names that begin with the *sh* sound. Ask them to write those names on the chalkboard. Help them with the spelling. Underline the beginning letter. If their names don't begin with *sh*, let them write their names anyway and discover that they do not begin with *sh*. Students can erase the names that don't begin with *sh* from the chalkboard. Names that begin with *sh* can be added to the newsprint sheet. Encourage students to keep adding names or words that begin or end with *sh* to the newsprint sheets.

4. Ask students to choose one *sh* word from the newsprint sheet to write in their spiral notebooks on page 83. Encourage illustration. This word will be their key word to remember the sound that *sh* makes.

5. Direct the students' attention to the exercise at the bottom of pupil page 83. Explain that you will dictate a list of words. If the word contains the *sh* sound, they should circle the *sh* beside the appropriate number. If the word does not contain the *sh* sound, they should mark an *X* over the letters. Dictate: *1. sun 2. wish 3. shop 4. sail 5. brushing 6. children 7. shiny 8. dishes 9. sheet.*

OBJECTIVE

Students will associate the letter symbol *th* with the appropriate sound.

PREPARATION

Bring the alphabet flash cards. Prepare a set of flash cards containing the following words: *thumb, mouth, bathtub, tenth, thimble, three.*

PRESENTATION

1. Ask students to name the letters in the boxes at the top of pupil page 84. Have them write the letters several times in their spiral notebooks on page 84.

2. Hold up the *thumb* flash card and say *thumb*. Emphasize the sound of the *th*. Ask the students to repeat the sound several times. Point from the flash card to the picture on pupil page 84 while repeating *thumb*. Ask the students to write the word in their spiral notebooks. Repeat this procedure with the other words and pictures on pupil page 84.

3. Ask students to raise their hands if their first or last names begin with the same sound heard in the words they just learned. Write those names on the *th* newsprint sheet. Ask if students know any other names that begin with the *th* sound. Ask them to write those names on the chalkboard. Help them with the spelling. Underline the beginning letter. If their names don't begin with *th*, let them write their names anyway and discover that they do not begin with *th*. Students can erase the names that don't begin with *th* from the chalkboard. Names that begin with *th* can be added to the newsprint sheet. Encourage students to keep adding names or words that begin or end with *th* to the newsprint sheet.

4. Ask students to choose one *th* word from the newsprint sheet to write on notebook page 84. Encourage illustration. This word will be their key word to remember the sound that *th* makes.

5. Direct the students' attention to the exercise at the bottom of pupil page 84. Explain that you will dictate a list of words. If the word begins with the *th* sound, they should circle the *th* beside the appropriate number. If the word does not begin with the *th* sound, they should mark an *X* over the letters. Dictate: *1. with 2. teeth 3. thick 4. town 5. chain 6. thin 7. moth 8. sand 9. happy.*

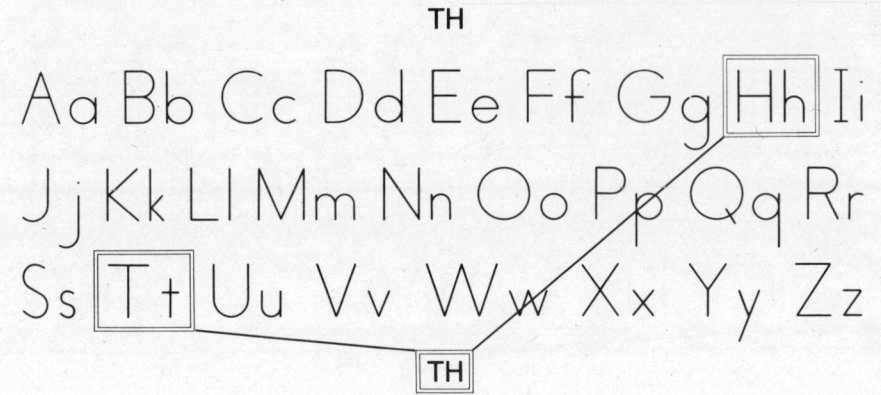

TH

Aa Bb Cc Dd Ee Ff Gg [Hh] Ii
Jj Kk Ll Mm Nn Oo Pp Qq Rr
Ss [Tt] Uu Vv Ww Xx Yy Zz
[TH]

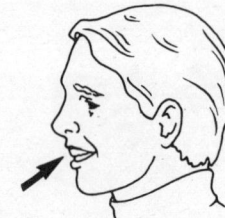
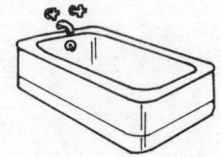

| thumb | mouth | bathtub |

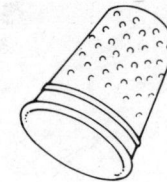

| tenth | thimble | three |

1. (th)   2. (th)   3. (th)
4. ⨉   5. ⨉   6. (th)
7. (th)   8. ⨉   9. ⨉

SH

ship

S

sip

---

1. *sock*

sh   ⓢ

2. *shoe*

⓼   s

3. *fish*

⓼   s

4. *dish*

⓼   s

5. *bus*

sh   ⓢ

6. *dishwasher*

⓼   s

7. *shave*

⓼   s

8. *sun*

sh   ⓢ

9. *six*

sh   ⓢ

85

OBJECTIVE

Students will differentiate between the sounds of *sh* and *s*.

PREPARATION

Make photocopied enlargements of the illustrations at the top of pupil page 85. Attach the illustrations to opposite sides of the chalkboard. Cut paper into strips for writing sentences.

PRESENTATION

1. Point to the ship at the top of pupil page 85 and then to the ship on the chalkboard. Say *ship* several times. Emphasize the sound of the *sh*. Do the same with *sip*.

2. Point to illustration #1 on pupil page 85. Say *sock* with an emphasis on the *s* sound. Ask the students whether the *s* in *sock* sounds like the *s* in *ship*. Does it sound like the *s* in *sip*? Model circling the correct response under the illustration. Ask the students to do the same in their texts. Repeat with the remaining illustrations, using the following words: *shoe, fish, dish, bus, dishwasher, shave, sun, six*.

3. Ask a student to put the words *sip* and *ship* on the appropriate newsprint sheets.

4. Create two teams. Ask the two team players to stand on either side of the chalkboard. Dictate words at random that contain either the *s* or the *sh* sounds. Have each player place a chalk mark under the illustration on the chalkboard with the same sound as the dictated word. Play to ten points.

5. Have the students create a Language Experience Story (LES) by asking the following questions: *How often do you use a dishwasher?* or *Do you ride the bus? Where? When?* In this LES, make suggestions to help students write complete sentences, but try not to change the meaning students intended. Ask them if the changes are acceptable. Have the students write the dialogues in their spiral notebooks on page 85.

OBJECTIVE

Students will differentiate between the sounds of *sh* and *ch*.

PREPARATION

Make photocopied enlargements of the illustrations at the top of pupil page 86. Attach the illustrations to opposite sides of the chalkboard. Cut paper into strips for writing sentences.

PRESENTATION

1. Point to the ships at the top of pupil page 86 and then to the ships on the chalkboard. Say *ships* several times. Emphasize the sound of the *sh*. Do the same with *chips*.

2. Point to illustration #1 on pupil page 86. Say *chain* with an emphasis on the *ch* sound. Ask the students whether the *ch* in *chain* sounds like the *sh* in *ship*. Does it sound like the *ch* in *chips*? Model circling the correct response under the illustration. Ask the students to do the same in their texts. Repeat with the remaining illustrations, using the following words: *chimney, shirt, fish, lunch, cheese, church, shovel, chicken.*

3. Ask a student to put the words *ships* and *chips* on the appropriate newsprint sheets.

4. Create two teams. Ask the two team players to stand on either side of the chalkboard. Dictate words at random containing either the *ch* or the *sh* sounds. Have each player place a chalk mark under the illustration on the chalkboard with the same sound as the dictated word. Play to ten points.

5. Have the students create a Language Experience Story (LES) by asking the following questions: *Does your house or apartment have a chimney? What is a chimney for? Who cleans the chimney? With what? A brush?* In this LES, make suggestions to help students write complete sentences, but try not to change the meaning students intended. Ask them if the changes are acceptable. Have the students write the dialogues in their spiral notebooks on page 86.

SH	CH

ships	chips

1. *chain*	2. *chimney*	3. *shirt*

sh (ch)	sh (ch)	(sh) ch
4. *fish*	5. *lunch*	6. *cheese*
	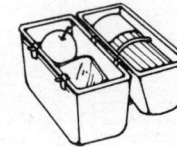	
(sh) ch	sh (ch)	sh (ch)
7. *church*	8. *shovel*	9. *chicken*

sh (ch)	(sh) ch	sh (ch)

T	TH
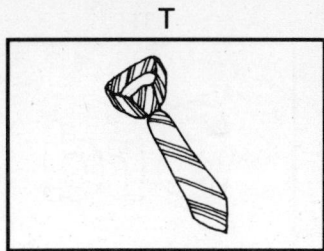	
tie	thirty

1. **thirteen**

t · (th)

2. **tent**

(t) · th

3. **thread**

t · (th)

4. **goat**

(t) · th

5. **bath**

t · (th)

6. **ten**

(t) · th

7. **thief**

t · (th)

8. **three**

t · (th)

9. **thermometer**

t · (th)

87

OBJECTIVE

Students will differentiate between the sounds of *t* and *th*.

PREPARATION

Make photocopied enlargements of the illustrations at the top of pupil page 87. Attach the illustrations to opposite sides of the chalkboard. Cut paper into strips for writing sentences.

PRESENTATION

1. Point to the *tie* at the top of pupil page 87 and then to the tie on the chalkboard. Say *tie* several times. Emphasize the sound of the *t*. Do the same with *thirty*.

2. Point to illustration #1 on pupil page 87. Say *thirteen* with an emphasis on the *th* sound. Ask the students whether the *th* in *thirteen* sounds like the *t* in *tie*. Does it sound like the *th* in *thirty*? Model circling the correct response under the illustration. Ask the students to do the same in their texts. Repeat with the remaining illustrations, using the following words: *tent, thread, goat, bath, ten, thief, three, thermometer*.

3. Ask a student to put the words *tie* and *thirty* on the appropriate newsprint sheets.

4. Create two teams. Ask the two team players to stand on either side of the chalkboard. Dictate words at random containing either the *t* or the *th* sound. Have each player place a chalk mark under the illustration on the chalkboard with the same sound as the dictated word. Play to ten points.

5. Have the students create a Language Experience Story (LES) by asking the following questions: *Are you thirsty? What kind of food makes you thirsty? What do you drink when you are thirsty?* In this LES, make suggestions to help students write complete sentences, but try not to change the meaning students intended. Ask them if the changes are acceptable. Have the students write the dialogues in their spiral notebooks on page 87.

OBJECTIVE

Students will differentiate between the sounds of *sh* and *th*.

PREPARATION

Make photocopied enlargements of the illustrations at the top of pupil page 88. Attach the illustrations to opposite sides of the chalkboard.

PRESENTATION

1. Point to the shirt at the top of pupil page 88 and then to the shirt on the chalkboard. Say *shirt* several times. Emphasize the sound of the *sh*. Do the same with *third*.

2. Point to illustration #1 on pupil page 88. Say *tooth* with an emphasis on the *th* sound. Ask the students whether the *th* in *tooth* sounds like the *th* in *third*. Does it sound like the *sh* in *shirt*? Model circling the correct response under the illustration. Ask the students to do the same in their texts. Repeat with the remaining illustrations, using the following words: *mushroom, shark, brush, toothpaste, trash, thief, shampoo, bath.*

3. Ask a student to put the words *shirt* and *third* on the appropriate newsprint sheets.

4. Create two teams. Ask the two team players to stand on either side of the chalkboard. Dictate words at random, containing either the *sh* or the *th* sound. Have each player place a chalk mark under the illustration on the chalkboard with the same sound as the dictated word. Play to ten points.

5. Have the students create a Language Experience Story (LES) by asking the following questions: *What time do you brush your teeth? What kind of toothpaste do you use?* In this LES, make suggestions to help students write complete sentences, but try not to change the meaning students intended. Ask them if the changes are acceptable. Have the students write the dialogues in their spiral notebooks on page 88.

SH — shirt

TH — 3rd — third

1. teeth — sh / (th)
2. mushroom — (sh) / th
3. shark — (sh) / th
4. brush — (sh) / th
5. toothpaste — sh / (th)
6. trash — (sh) / th
7. thief — sh / (th)
8. shampoo — (sh) / th
9. bath — sh / (th)

S	TH
	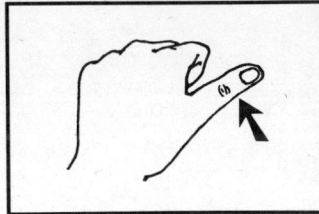
sink	thumb

1. **mouth**    s   (th)

2. **saw** 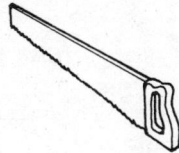   (s)   th

3. **teeth**   s   (th)

4. **sailboat**    (s)   th

5. **mouse**    (s)   th

6. **thirty**   30   s   (th)

7. **bathtub** 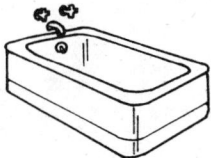   s   (th)

8. **sock**    (s)   th

9. **ninth**   9th   s   (th)

OBJECTIVE

Students will differentiate between the sounds of *s* and *th*.

PREPARATION

Make photocopied enlargements of the illustrations at the top of pupil page 89. Attach the illustrations to opposite sides of the chalkboard. Cut paper into strips for writing sentences.

PRESENTATION

1. Point to the sink at the top of pupil page 89 and then to the sink on the chalkboard. Say *sink* several times. Emphasize the sound of the *s*. Do the same with *thumb*.

2. Point to illustration #1 on pupil page 89. Say *mouth* with an emphasis on the *th* sound. Ask the students whether the *th* in *mouth* sounds like the *th* in *thumb*. Does it sound like the *s* in *sink*? Model circling the correct response under the illustration. Ask the students to do the same in their texts. Repeat with the remaining illustrations, using the following words: *saw, teeth, sailboat, mouse, thirty, bathtub, sock, ninth.*

3. Ask a student to put the words *sink* and *thumb* on the appropriate newsprint sheets.

4. Create two teams. Ask the two team players to stand on either side of the chalkboard. Dictate words at random containing either the *s* or the *th* sound. Have each player place a chalk mark under the illustration on the chalkboard with the same sound as the dictated word. Play to ten points.

5. Have the students create a Language Experience Story (LES) by asking the following questions: *Do you have a saw? What is a saw for? What other tools do you have?* In this LES, make suggestions to help students write complete sentences, but try not to change the meaning students intended. Ask them if the changes are acceptable. Have the students write the dialogues in their spiral notebooks on page 89.

OBJECTIVE

Students will distinguish among the sounds of *ch*, *s*, *sh*, *t*, and *th*.

PREPARATION

Cut paper into strips for writing sentences. Photocopy pupil page 90.

PRESENTATION

1. Pronounce the following words. Ask students to write in the blanks the letters which represent the sounds they hear. Demonstrate on pupil page 90. Dictate:

1. chew	15. then	19. sun
2. shut	16. path	30. chain
3. shop	17. sick	31. death
4. but	18. sew	32. time
5. much	19. ten	33. cheese
6. shy	20. theme	34. sing
7. cashed	21. crash	35. shoe
8. with	22. ouch	36. silk
9. save	23. children	37. bat
10. thank	24. coat	38. shine
11. start	25. both	39. salt
12. rent	26. fish	40. cash
13. with	27. show	
14. shelf	28. hit	

2. Distribute the photocopied pages. Repeat the exercise following the procedure above. Have the students check their answers with the information in their texts.

3. Have the students create a Language Experience Story (LES) by asking the following questions: *Do you like to sing? What songs do you know? Teach me a song.* In this LES, make suggestions to help students write complete sentences, but try not to change the meaning students intended. Ask them if the changes are acceptable. Have the students write the dialogues in their spiral notebooks on page 90.

---

ch s sh t th

1. _c_ _h_ e w
2. _s_ _h_ u t
3. _s_ _h_ o p
4. b u _t_
5. m u _c_ _h_
6. _s_ _h_ y
7. c a _s_ _h_ e d
8. w i _t_ _h_
9. _s_ a v e
10. _t_ _h_ a n k
11. s t a r _t_
12. r e n _t_
13. w i _s_ _h_
14. _s_ _h_ e l f
15. _t_ _h_ i n
16. p a _t_ _h_
17. _s_ i c k
18. _s_ e w
19. _t_ e n
20. _t_ _h_ e m e
21. c r a _s_ _h_
22. o u _c_ _h_
23. _c_ _h_ i l d r e n
24. c o a _t_
25. b o _t_ _h_
26. f i _s_ _h_
27. _s_ _h_ o w
28. h i _t_
29. _s_ u n
30. _c_ _h_ a i n
31. d e a _t_ _h_
32. _t_ i m e
33. _c_ _h_ e e s e
34. _s_ i n g
35. _s_ _h_ o e
36. _s_ i l k
37. b a _t_
38. _s_ _h_ i n e
39. _s_ a l t
40. c a _s_ _h_

	ch	s	sh	th
1.	(says)	shop	shoot	shed
B 2.	cheek	(city)	chop	check
3.	thick	thought	(tell)	thing

1.	with	bath	math	(mash)
E 2.	March	(trash)	beach	inch
3.	want	light	boot	(cloth)

1. ___s___ ___h___ ell

2. ___t___ ___h___ ree

3. boa ___t___

4. ___s___ ock

5. bru ___s___ ___h___

6. ba ___t___ ___h___ tub

7. ___c___ ___h___ ain

8. bu ___s___

9. ___t___ oe

OBJECTIVE

Students will review distinguishing among the sounds of *ch*, *s*, *sh*, *t*, and *th*.

PREPARATION

Cut paper into strips for writing sentences.

PRESENTATION

1. At the top of pupil page 91, ask students to circle the one word in each line that begins (*B*) with a sound that is different than the rest of the words. Students should circle: 1. *says* 2. *city* 3. *tell*. Then ask students to circle the one word in each line that ends (*E*) with a sound that is different than the rest of the words. Students should circle: 1. *mash* 2. *trash* 3. *cloth*. Variation: For students who need a simpler lesson, ask them to circle the words that begin and end with the same sound.

2. At the bottom of pupil page 91, ask students to study the pictures chosen from vocabulary already learned. Ask them to write the correct letter or letters in the blanks to complete each word:

1. *shell*	2. *three*	3. *boat*
4. *sock*	5. *brush*	6. *bathtub*
7. *chain*	8. *bus*	9. *toe*

3. Have the students create a Language Experience Story (LES) by asking the following questions: *Have you ever been in a boat? What kind of boat? Where did you go?* In this LES, make suggestions to help students write complete sentences, but try not to change the meaning students intended. Ask them if the changes are acceptable. Have the students write the dialogues in their spiral notebooks on page 91.

OBJECTIVE

Students will distinguish among the sounds of *ch*, *s*, *sh*, *t* , and *th*.

PREPARATION

Cut paper into strips for writing sentences. Bring lined paper.

PRESENTATION

1. For the first activity, ask the students to circle the letter or letters they hear in each word. Ask them to mark an *X* over the letters that represent the sounds they don't hear. Dictate these words:

SH:	1. rash	2. silly	3. check
CH:	1. church	2. choose	3. shake
TH:	1. mouth	2. eat	3. ninth
T:	1. tell	2. cut	3. thumb
S:	1. sign	2. shine	3. push

2. In the middle of the page, say the names of each picture. Ask students to repeat the word after you. Then ask them to circle the letter or letters that represent the sound they hear in each word. Ask them to mark an *X* over the letter or letters that have a different sound.

3. At the bottom of the page, pronounce the following words clearly and ask students to write in the blanks the letters which represent the sound they hear. Dictate: *1. thank 2. time 3. math 4. fish 5. children 6. sheep 7. much 8. bus 9. sit.*

4. Have the students create a Language Experience Story (LES) by asking the following questions: *Did you enjoy the class? What did you like about the class?* In this LES, make suggestions to help students write complete sentences, but try not to change the meaning students intended. Ask them if the changes are acceptable. Have the students write the dialogues in their spiral notebooks on page 92.

5. Ask students to write their names, today's date, and the time on notebook page 92. Make corrections if needed. Distribute the lined paper. Ask students to copy the LES and write their names, today's date, and the time at the top. Make a collection of *all* the LES stories and put them in a booklet. Ask a student to number the pages of the book. Ask whose story is at the beginning, middle, and end of the book. Make a cover and ask students to select a title. Choose a student to write the title on the cover and ask students to write their signatures on the cover. Put the booklet on display in a hall or other community area.

Blackline Masters: Notes to the teacher

Below are suggestions for using each of the extra practice pages included in this *Teacher's Edition*.

1. and 2. Use these pages to make flash cards for reviewing the letter sounds on pupil pages 1-7. Photocopy and enlarge the Blacklines # 1 and #2. Cut out all of the picture and letter flash cards. Put the picture cards on one side of the table and the letter cards on the other side. Have students play Concentration by turning over one card from each set. If the picture begins with the same sound as the letter indicated on the letter flash card, students receive one point.

3. and 4. Use these pages to review vowel and consonant sounds from pupil pages 8-46. Tell the students you will dictate a word. On Blackline #3, have the students write the beginning consonant they hear on the line below the picture. On Blackline #4, have the student write the vowel they hear in the middle of the word. Dictate:

   Blackline 3: *bat, razor, deer, mule, watch, hand, cup, grapes*

   Blackline 4: *coat, cat, leaf, nest, fan, egg, duck, bus*

5. Use with pupil pages 47-49 to review the sounds of C, G, E, and O. Carefully pronounce the words on each line. On the first four lines, ask students to circle the word that does not begin with the same sound. On lines 5-8, ask students to circle the word containing the different vowel sound.

6. Use to reinforce the concept of beginning, end, and middle on pupil pages 50-64. Name each picture. Ask the students to circle the words after the picture that contain the same beginning, end, or middle sounds.

7. Use as a review of the days of the week and their abbreviations. Ask the students to fill in the blanks with the appropriate abbreviations.

8. Use as a review of the months of the year and of cardinal numbers. Ask the students to match each month to its appropriate number.

9. Use as a review for writing dates. Have each student ask for and write down the birth dates of six other classmates.

10. Use as a review of time. Ask the students to draw hands on their clocks to indicate the following times: 10:45, 11:30, 3:15, 6:45, 8:00.

11. Use as a review of A.M. and P.M. Ask the students to write A.M. or P.M. under each picture, as appropriate.

12. and 13. Use as a review of digraphs and the letters S and T.
    Follow same preparation procedures as for Blacklines #1 and #2.

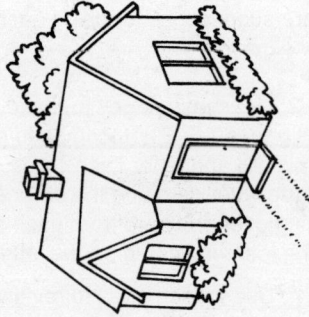

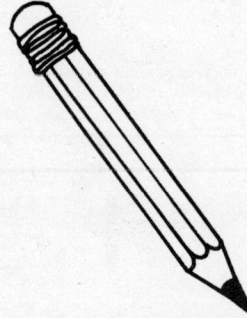

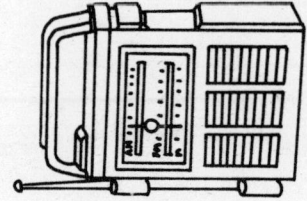

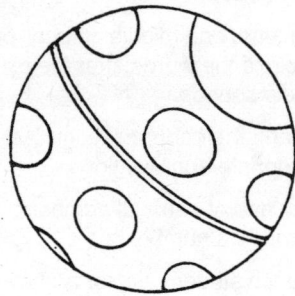

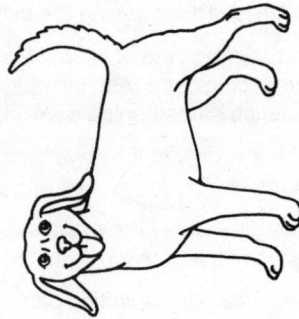

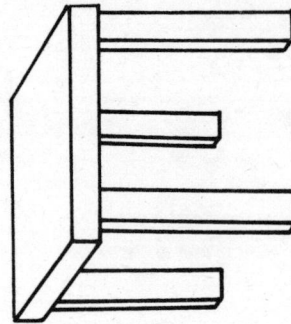

1

94   © 1991 Steck-Vaughn Company. *Entry to English Literacy*

NAME _____

B	D	T	K
C	H	P	R

© 1991 Steck-Vaughn Company. *Entry to English Literacy* **95**

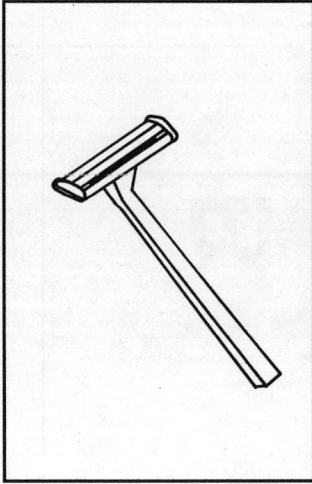
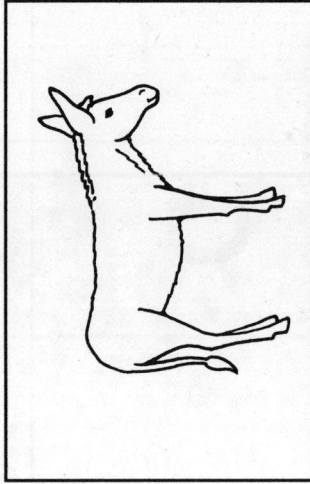
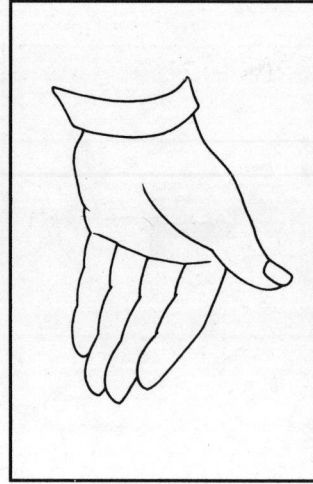

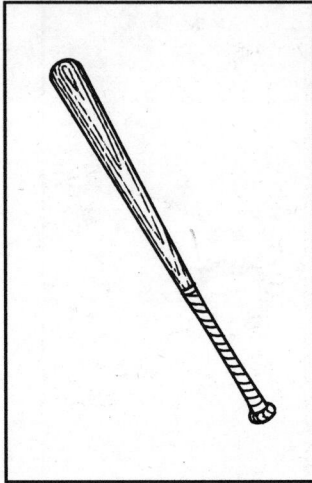
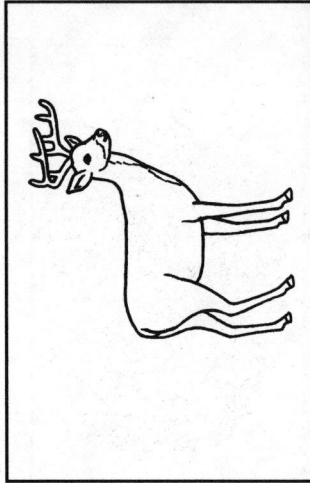

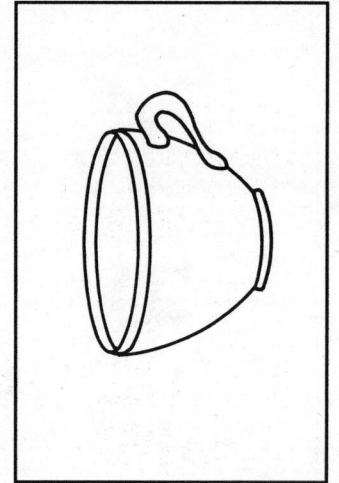

 © 1991 Steck-Vaughn Company. *Entry to English Literacy*

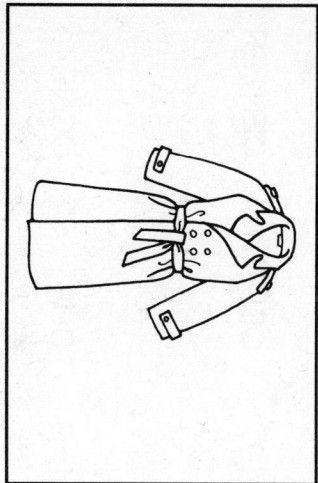

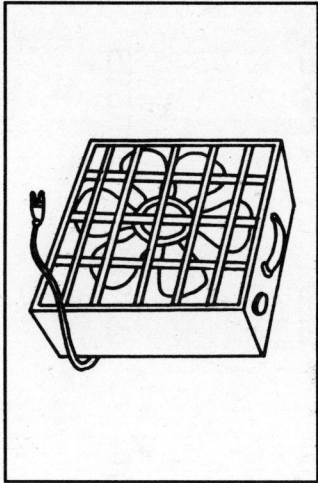

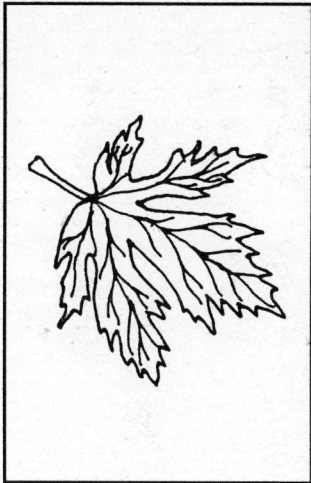

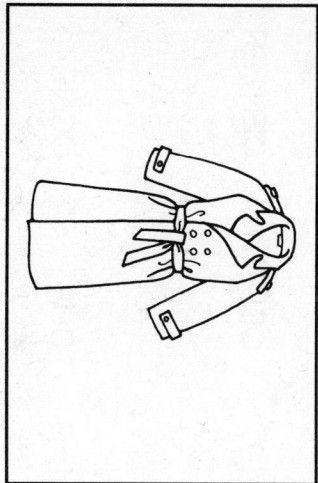

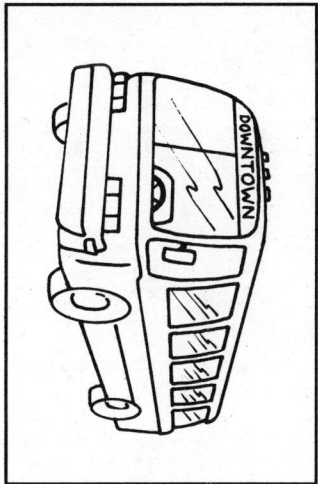

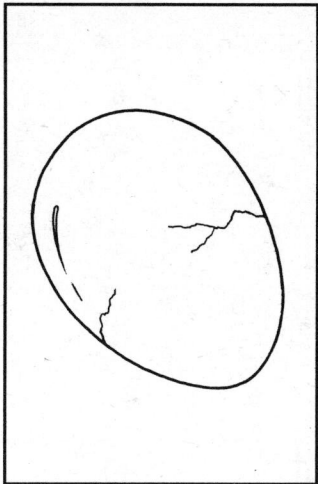

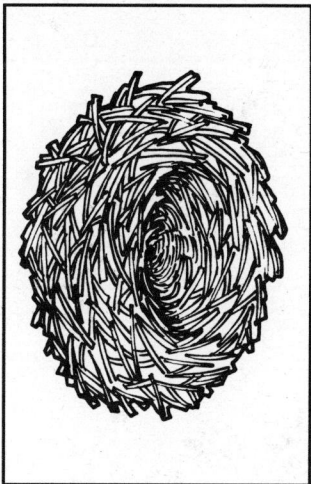

NAME _____

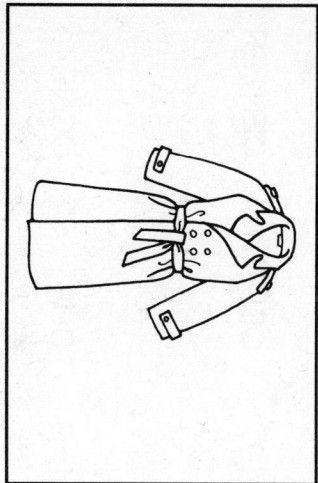

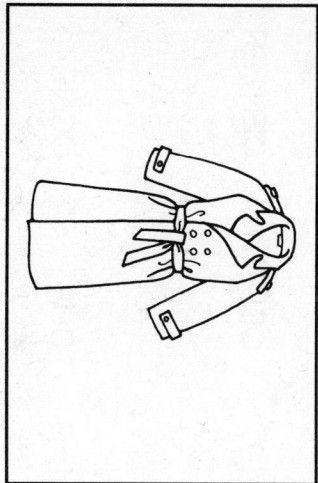

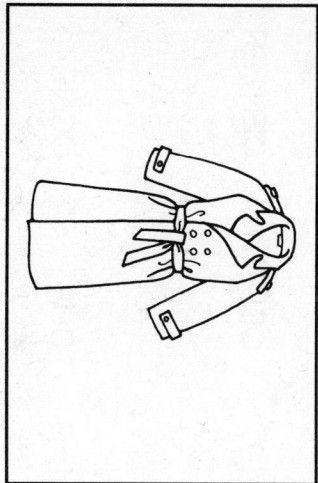

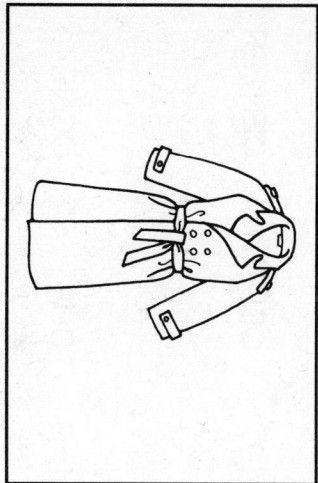

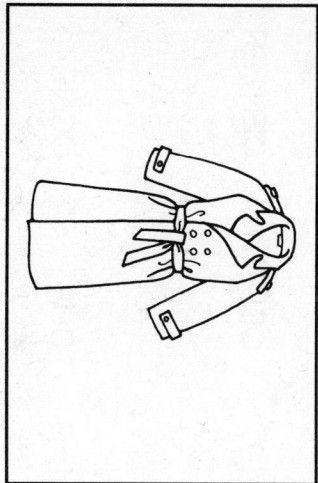

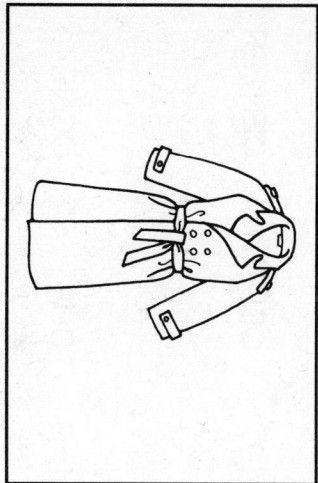

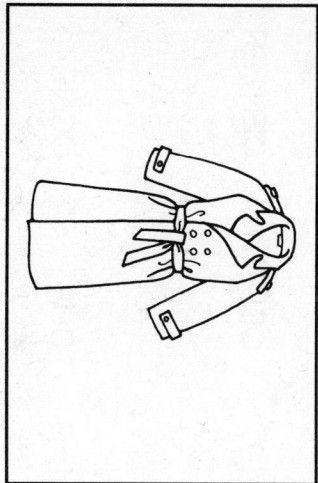

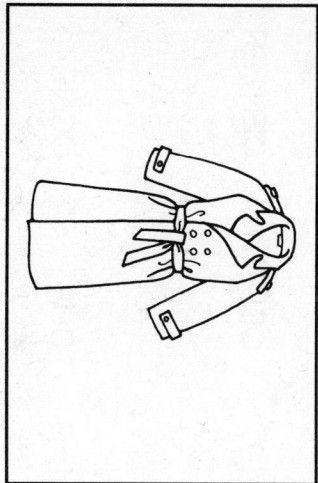

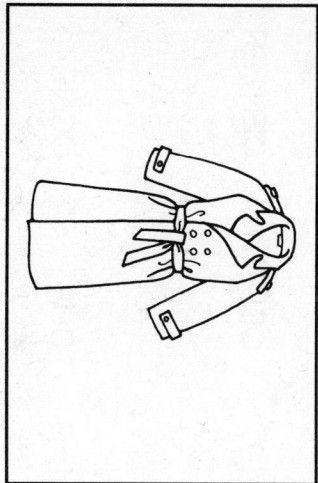

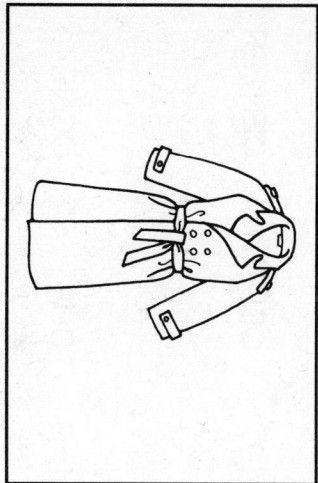

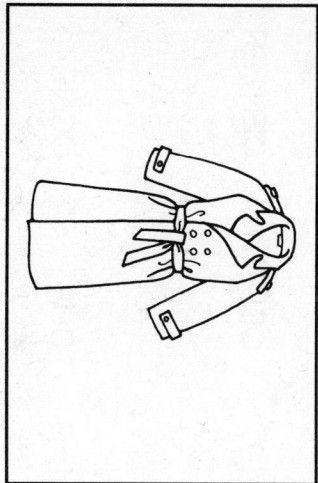

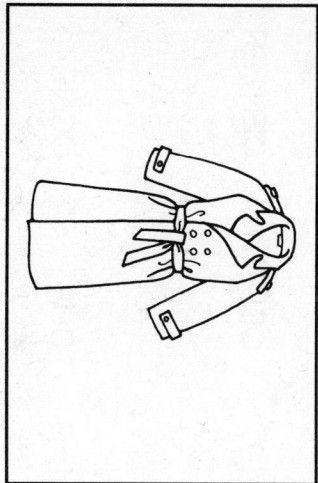

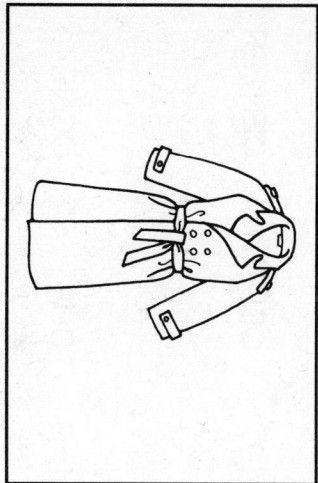

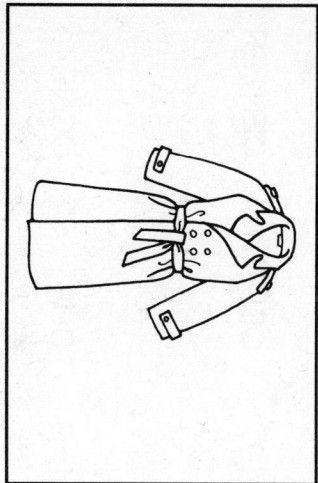

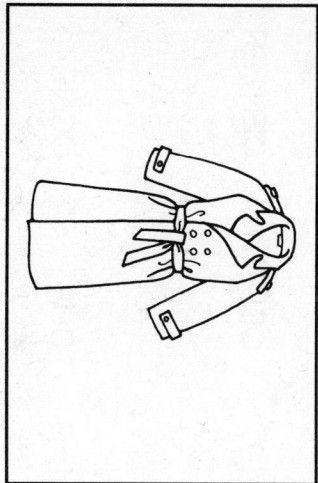

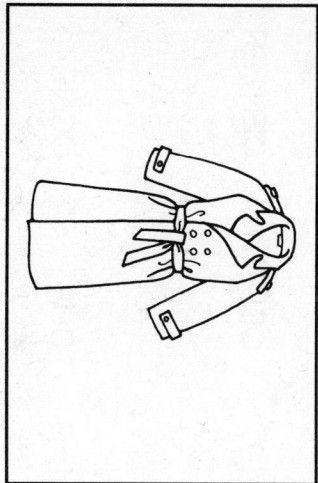

4

© 1991 Steck-Vaughn Company. *Entry to English Literacy* 97

NAME _____

CEREAL	CEILING	COFFEE	CIGAR	CELERY	CENTER	CIRCLE
CAT	COLD	CASH	CITY	CUP	CONE	CANDLE
GIANT	GIRAFFE	GOAT	GENERAL	GYPSY	GYM	GEL
GET	GOLD	GATHER	GAS	GEM	GAME	GATE
BEE	KEY	KNEE	SEED	BED	LEAVE	GREED
HEAD	FED	MEAN	NEST	GUESS	PRESS	FELL
BOX	FOX	SOCKS	COAT	LOST	MOSS	TOP
GOAT	LOAD	BONE	COUGH	DOUGH	HOLD	BLOW

 © 1991 Steck-Vaughn Company. *Entry to English Literacy*

NAME _____

B

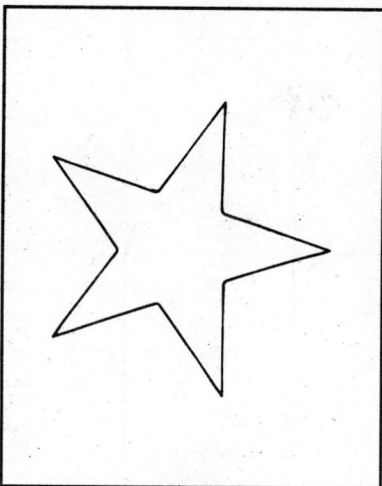

SAND ZOO BUS JAR

E

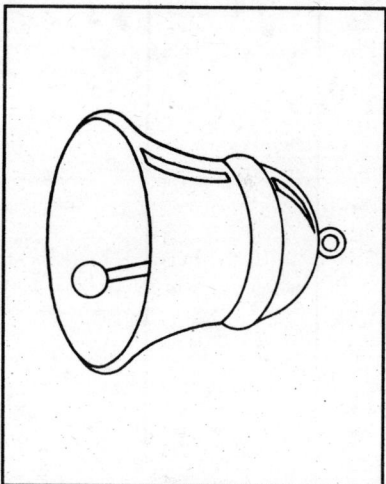

RED PULL ZIP IF

M

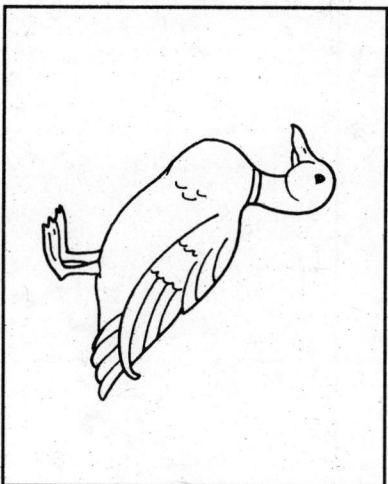

BUS SIN US CALL

© 1991 Steck-Vaughn Company. *Entry to English Literacy* **99**

7

NAME _____

SUNDAY |

MONDAY |

TUESDAY |

WEDNESDAY |

THURSDAY |

FRIDAY |

SATURDAY |

 © 1991 Steck-Vaughn Company. *Entry to English Literacy*

8

NAME

JANUARY	7
FEBRUARY	8
MARCH	9
APRIL	5
MAY	12
JUNE	1
JULY	6
AUGUST	2
SEPTEMBER	10
OCTOBER	3
NOVEMBER	11
DECEMBER	4

NAME _____

9

NAME _____ DATE OF BIRTH

NAME _____ DATE OF BIRTH

NAME _____ DATE OF BIRTH

NAME _____ DATE OF BIRTH

NAME _____ DATE OF BIRTH

NAME _____ DATE OF BIRTH

NAME

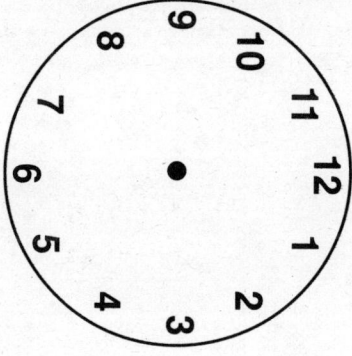

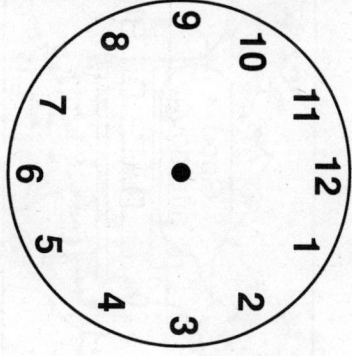

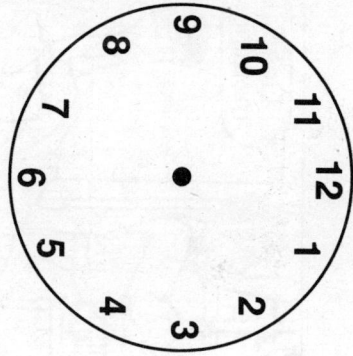

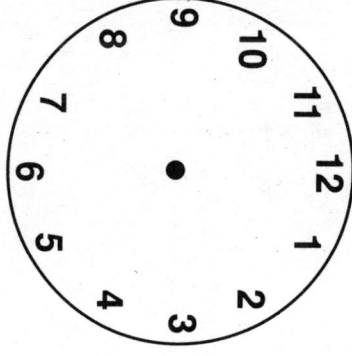

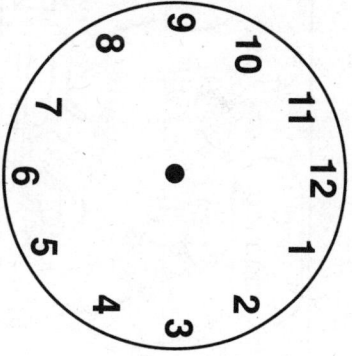

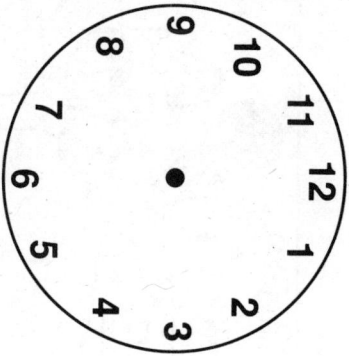

© 1991 Steck-Vaughn Company. *Entry to English Literacy* **103**

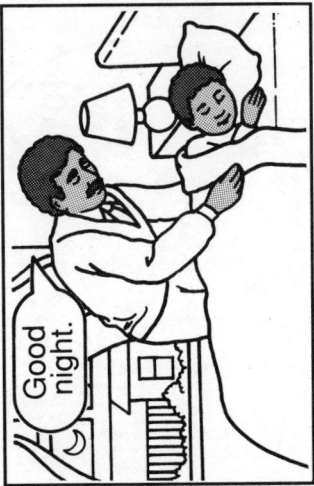

NAME _____

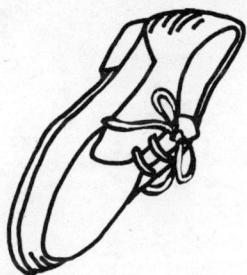

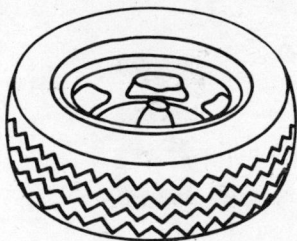

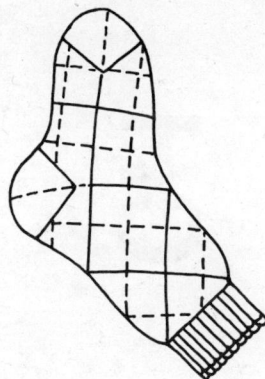

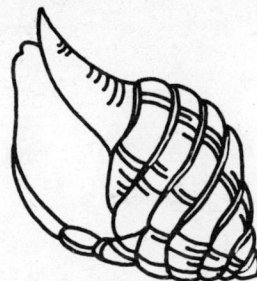

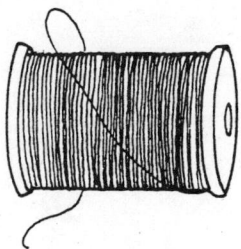

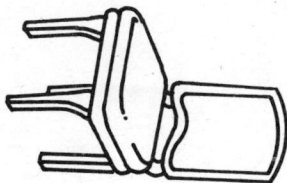

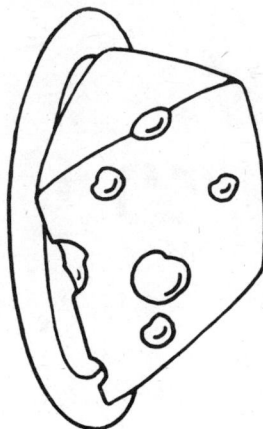

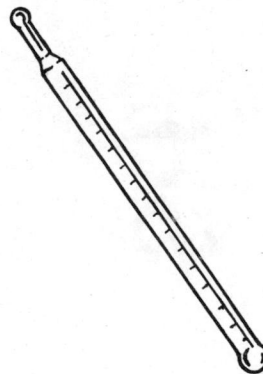

© 1991 Steck-Vaughn Company. *Entry to English Literacy* **105**

NAME

13

TH	CH	CH	TH
SH	S	T	SH